WE CANNOT BUT TELL

A Practical Guide to HEART TO HEART EVANGELISM

Ross Tooley

Publishing
A Ministry of Youth With A Mission
P.O. Box 55787, Seattle, WA 98155

WE CANNOT BUT TELL

A Practical Guide to HEART TO HEART EVANGELISM

We Cannot But Tell

Published by YWAM Publishing, a division of Youth With A Mission; P.O. Box 55787; Seattle, Washington 98155.

ISBN 0-927545-42-X

Table of Contents

Foreword

When I first met Ross Tooley, I was impressed with his zeal, his commitment to the Lord, and his faith to launch new things for God. In his than 26 years with Youth With A Mission (YWAM), I have had ample opportunity to observe him. I have worked alongside him in various capacities—even in hut-to-hut evangelism among Hindus in Fiji.

Ross is a missionary pioneer who has had extensive experience in frontline, eye-to-eye evangelism. Many years ago, Ross was with other YWAMers in the Kingdom of Tonga during the coronation celebration for their new king. Following a fireworks display one night, Ross decided to start a street meeting. So many people gathered around that Ross climbed onto the base of a flagpole to continue addressing the crowd. Hundreds heard the Gospel that night, and many responded to the altar calls. Scenes like this have been repeated many, many times over the years as Ross has ministered around the world.

At one of Billy Graham's conferences for itinerant evangelists, I met a man who is the leader of a missionary organization in the Philippines. He shared how he was won to Christ by Ross Tooley in the Philippines some 15 years prior, and owes the ministry he has today to Ross's input into his life. Other leaders could share this same testimony. Ross has also had a ministry of motivating people into full-time missions through the years. Many Christian leaders and pastors are in the work of the Lord today as a result of having worked with him or having listened to him speak.

As a teacher of God's Word, Ross shares from a wealth of experience and relationship with God. When it comes to evangelism, he knows what he's talking about. I highly recommend Ross and his book for your edification.

Loren Cunningham
President, Youth With A Mission

Author's Preface
New Edition

This book has been written for all Christians. It starts by giving reasons why we should be involved in witnessing, then covers the whole spectrum of evangelism right through to leading someone to Christ. It gives tips for doing follow-up, and suggests instructions that should be given immediately to new Christians.

But while this book has been written for the general Body of Christ, I have also had in mind a more specific group of Christians. I've included some guidelines for those witnessing to people who know little about Christianity—like atheists and those of New Age thought—and for those sharing with people from religious backgrounds outside (and sometimes opposed to) the Christian faith.

For the sake of clarity, the book is now divided into four parts: *Preparing Our Hearts* (before we start witnessing), *Presenting the Message* (while we are witnessing), *Preserving the Results* (after we have witnessed), and *Some Other Considerations* (extending our effectiveness).

The last section of the book, which has been added to this new edition, tells how to write your own testimony tract, and gives some important overall statements about evangelism.

In the discussion about cross-cultural issues (Chapter 17), I have itemized a number of issues where Westerners and non-Westerners are culturally different. As we witness cross-culturally, our evangelism may penetrate to a deeper and more meaningful level if we understand these areas.

This information is not merely for those planning to serve overseas. With present increases in immigration, your next-door neighbor might be from Africa, Latin America, or Asia. For this reason, I recommend you carefully consider the contents of Chapter Seventeen. As you read my examples you'll probably recognize your old friend from school, your former work mate, or the people in a community near you. My aim is to help you understand ways to better evangelize your neighbors who are from minority groups native to North America and the Third World.

But if you do plan to work for the Lord abroad one day, I trust you will find much in the book that will be helpful. I have worked in missions for almost 27 years on four continents—Asia, Europe, North America, and the South Pacific. While I advocate cultural awareness and flexibility, some things do not change: Every person must acknowledge a God who was not created, that His Son Jesus died and rose again for our sin, and that we are required to repent in order to know God. But my experience has taught me that there are *a variety of ways* to go about preaching this message—ways which are more effective in one culture than in another.

This new edition has been subjected to a thorough rewrite, and incorporates the truths I have been learning as I continue to witness. I heartily commend you to God as you read, and I pray His blessing upon you as you venture through this book.

Ross Tooley
May, 1993

Section I

Preparing Our Hearts

1

Why Personal Evangelism?

I looked at my watch. *Oh, no!* I thought. In just ten minutes, the banks would close and stay shut for the next three days.

I was in Colombo, Sri Lanka, and I needed to cash traveler's checks on behalf of the Christian group I was traveling with. It could prove awkward for the entire team if we were to run out of Sri Lankan rupees over the coming holiday. Though I wasn't very close to the bank, I decided to make a dash for it.

I ran down the street and jumped on the next big red double-decker bus I saw. I paused to catch my breath, then began looking for a place to sit. I perched nervously on the edge of a seat, looking at my watch, just hoping that I would make it to the bank on time.

After what seemed an eternity, the bus shuddered to a stop near the Bank of Ceylon. But as I jumped out and glanced toward the bank, my heart sank. The iron gate had been drawn closed, and a young man guarded the entrance. I ran over and appealed to the young man to let me in, but he refused. Now desperate, and feeling responsible for my oversight, I asked to see the manager.

"Do you know the manager?" The young man's eyes opened wide in amazement. I didn't want to tell him that I'd never met the manager, so all I did was repeat my request. It worked, for he slid the iron gate to one side, directed me up the stairs, and ushered me into the manager's office.

The manager, a neatly dressed, middle-aged man with a slightly sad expression on his face, sat at a wooden desk in the small room. After I explained what I needed, he asked me to be seated while an officer changed the traveler's checks for me.

"What brings you to Sri Lanka?" he asked. I told him that I was with some Christians sharing our message as we traveled in Asia.

"Who is paying your way?" Of course, a banker would be interested in that aspect of the trip! I explained that we were each responsible for our own expenses, and that some of us looked to God for that supply.

Seeing that the topic of Christianity had been raised, and sensing that the timing was right, I asked him a question which I hoped would lead into a witnessing situation. As naturally as possible, I inquired, "Are you interested in spiritual matters?"

From his answer, he didn't appear very interested, although he did talk about going to church. As we chatted back and forth about Christian things, I found myself searching for a way to make clear that by itself, his church background was not enough to assure salvation. Suddenly I had an inspiration.

Leaning forward just a little, I courteously asked, "Would you say, then, that you are a friend of God's?"

I was quite unprepared for his response. Right there in the bank, this otherwise dignified banker raised both arms above his head and exclaimed, "I would give anything in the world to be God's friend, and to have peace of mind!"

From his outburst, I knew he should be interested in the Gospel. Yet as we continued to talk, there seemed to be no indication that he wanted to give his life completely over to the Lord.

Finally, a clerk walked into the office and handed me the Sri Lankan rupees in exchange for my traveler's checks. I was disappointed that the conversation hadn't gone as deep as I had hoped after the manager's outburst, but I was thankful nonetheless that changing money in a developing nation takes time. The fifteen minutes or so of waiting had given me an opportunity to witness to this man in a meaningful way.

But I hated to leave it at that; he had opened his heart to me. *Shouldn't I ask if I could see him again?* I decided to take the plunge.

The result was an invitation for my wife and me to have dinner with Melville and his wife after the holidays. I left his office and bounded down the stairs two at a time, rejoicing that once again a routine, everyday affair had turned into a witnessing opportunity.

A week later, my wife Margaret and I sat down to a meal with

Melville and his wife at their home. They welcomed us with gracious hospitality and served us crab which was so spicy hot that we had to eat lots of rice and bananas to cool our burning mouths.

Melville and Mavis lived in a house that was comfortable by Sri Lankan standards, but was not lavish. After the meal, we retired to an area near the dining room for tea.

Since Melville and his wife came from a nominal Christian background, we were able to share the Scriptures with them both. At the end of the evening, Melville bought one of the New Testaments our team was selling. Before we left, we invited them to come to some special meetings we were holding in a local church.

The evening Melville came to our meeting, my sermon focused on the awfulness of sin and the cruel death of Christ that was needed to provide a way for the world to know God. When I gave the call to become a Christian, Melville came and knelt for prayer.

But it wasn't just my message that had made an impact. Much later, Melville told me what was going on in his life at that time.

Melville felt that he was being cheated financially by those around him, and he was becoming very bitter. Some of his friends had even suggested that he hire a killer to get rid of those cheating him. At the time we met, Melville's bitterness (and the depression that accompanied it) was so strong that he was willing to do almost anything to be free of the burden on his shoulders. Of course, he realized later that his real need was to get to know God as his Father.

Melville shared with me that our time in his home, plus the testimony of the team paying their way to share the Gospel, showed him a relationship of love to God that he had never seen. He knew that this love relationship with God must be real, and he wanted it.

We have kept in touch with Melville over the last twenty years, and have stayed with him in his home as we've passed through Sri Lanka. On one occasion, he obtained two months' leave of absence from the bank and traveled to the Philippines where Margaret and I were stationed. He spent those months sharing his testimony and going with an evangelistic team to the highlands north of our city. After that, he often visited nearby YWAM bases when he was on bank business abroad, and eventually he went through a YWAM

Discipleship Training School.

Melville certainly is a different man from the one I first met in the bank. How wonderful that a simple question like, "Are you interested in spiritual things?" had led to his eventual conversion.

A lot of this book is simply attempting to answer this question: How do we share our faith with people in ways that they will *appreciate and respond to?*

Witnessing for Christ is a fulfilling experience, and has its own special rewards. Whether it was a bank manager, a housewife thinking about burning down her home, the radical university student who is now a pastor, or a young lady on board an airline flight, everyone I have led to the Lord holds a special place in my heart.

To lay a foundation for the rest of the book, let's take a look at some of the compelling reasons why we should be involved in the activity called "witnessing."

It's God's will for our lives

I once heard the story of a British doctor on vacation in the Middle East. With hardly a care in the world, he was riding a train, enjoying his holiday, and certainly had no premonition of what lay literally around the next corner. The train began swaying violently, and the doctor desperately grabbed hold of one of the iron bars that ran alongside the window by his seat. As he held on grimly, he could hardly believe what he saw out the window. The carriages ahead were snaking their way through the field to the side of the tracks! The awful reality sank in when the train came to a clanging halt. For a brief moment there was only silence. But that soon gave way to sounds of groaning and shouting, which became louder and louder.

Shaken, the doctor looked around. No one was hurt near where he had been sitting. He managed to jump out of his compartment to the track below, and hurried alongside the wrecked train with its twisted cars. Wounded people were now emerging from the chaos. Both inside the carriages and beside the train lay human beings, hurting, bleeding, and dying.

It finally became too much for him, and he cried out in anguish: "My instruments! My instruments! If only I had my instruments! I could save these people!"

God must say the same thing at times. As He looks down upon a world of chaos brought about by man's inhumanity to man, He feels deep within His loving heart an even more profound anguish than the doctor's. His instruments to spread His message and thus bring about change are, of course, dedicated Christians. We are to move out into the sea of human need around us in loving obedience to His will.

It is a God of both love and justice who tells us,"Go into all the world and preach the good news to all creation" (Mark 16:15).

Showing love for people through personal evangelism demonstrates what God is like

Many today carry in their hearts deep-seated frustrations, fears, and wounds. It may be some horrifying experience or an injustice that has been dealt them. It could be loneliness or boredom. Whatever the case, the response of these people to the Gospel usually will depend on whether we really care about them. Jesus, the greatest personal evangelist of all time, showed us this.

Jesus was on the dusty road with His disciples one day, traveling from Judea on a three-day journey to Galilee. He had decided to take the route through a region inhabited by people of mixed Jewish and Gentile blood who were called *Samaritans.*

The antagonism between Jews and Samaritans was great. In fact, the Samaritans had once denied Jesus and His party lodging for the night. In response, James and John asked Jesus for permission to call down fire upon them (Luke 9:54). Anger toward the Samaritans seethed even in the breasts of Jesus' disciples—an animosity that reflected their cultural bias.

But on this particular trip through Samaria (John 4:3-42), Jesus, tired from His journey, stopped at Sychar and sat by an old well while the disciples went to get food. As He rested, a Samaritan woman came to the well to draw water.

How should Jesus react in the presence of one of these "despised people"? If He wanted to show interest and concern as a personal evangelist should, He faced definite problems as far as fitting in with the norms of His society. Should He speak to her?

In the first place, as a Jew, Jesus was supposed to have no unnecessary dealings with a Samaritan. Second, He would be considered ceremonially unclean if He were to quench his middle-of-the-day thirst using a Samaritan cup. Third, it would be unthinkable for Him to have anything to do with this woman, who was living in an adulterous relationship. But for Jesus, it was more important to demonstrate His love than to conform to the ungodly aspects of His society.

"Do you think you could let me drink out of your dipping container?" He asked politely.

The woman was astounded. Drawing her shawl a little closer to her face, she responded: "But You're a Jew, and I am a Samaritan woman. How can You ask me for a drink?"

This is how Jesus opened the conversation with a woman who had failed in five marriages and who must have been minus 500 on the self-esteem scale. He did not scold her, but spoke to her kindly, thus increasing her sense of self-worth. By showing interest and concern, Jesus wooed this woman to faith without compromising the commandment against adultery, which He upheld.

Then something happened as this lady became excited about Christ. Instead of denying Jesus and His disciples hospitality, the other Samaritans actually urged Him to stay in the village! The Bible tells us that many others came to faith during His two days in that village.

What an unprecedented outreach on Samaritan soil! How excited Jesus must have been to overcome the Samaritans' prejudice, and illustrate to His disciples how to evangelize in a caring way. At the same time, He had shown the Samaritans what God is really like. And it all started when Jesus showed interest in one lowly person—something that you and I can easily do.

We may worry about not knowing what to say when we witness, but we can all help love people into the Kingdom! The world would be won faster if we would all follow Jesus' example and demonstrate what God is like by personally presenting the Gospel.

Questions can be answered easier by personal evangelism

There is a sense in which we are called as Christians to clear away the objections that men have against serving the Lord—even though in the final analysis, no one has any excuse for the rejection of God (Romans 1:20). But the devil does manage to fool some people into thinking that they do have a good argument. We must expose the error of their thinking graciously. To do this, we need the leading of the Holy Spirit, and at times, the Holy Spirit's gifts.

When we don't answer people's questions satisfactorily, it can sometimes serve to confirm them in their unbelief. But a man full of honest questions is not always free to share his doubts in a public meeting. That's why personal evangelism is such an important part of Christianity.

All are not able to attend Christian meetings to hear the Gospel

Due to social customs and other difficulties related to location—especially in the non-Western World—some people just cannot attend Christian meetings. Others, of course, simply refuse to come to any Christian gathering.

So evangelism, as Jesus intended, was to meet people and win them on their own ground—at their businesses, in their homes, at the office, by the beach, or while traveling by public transportation. We should be reaching both friends and strangers for Christ during our routine life—as well as those times when we'll join organized witnessing drives into the parks, streets, jails, or hospitals. There is even a case for going house to house in areas, as some people, many who are handicapped, are confined to home.

Not everyone can read Christian literature

There is no doubt that the printed page has power to attract people's attention, to bring conviction and hope, and to lead people to Christ—even in hostile circumstances. K.K. Alavi's story is a case in point. As a Muslim youth, his mind could not escape the truths of God's Word which had been conveyed to him through a booklet he had once bought in a town where Christians were witnessing. Despite persecution from his family, including fierce beatings, God's Word burned into Alavi's consciousness and stayed there through the years until he eventually came to Christ. [1]

Yet even literature has its limitations. In our media-oriented world, not everybody cares to read. Even in the European nation of Portugal, 20 percent of the adult population cannot read or write. That figure climbs to above 50 percent in many African countries, and to 80 percent or more in other places. Therefore, the effectiveness of literature (which we should use to the maximum) is severely limited in many countries around the world.

In addition to illiteracy, the fact that many people have never seen a Bible or other piece of Christian literature in their own language demonstrates why we cannot rely on literature alone to evangelize the world.

Recently, my oldest son, Mark, returned from a trip to Albania and shared how he'd met Christians who had never seen any portion of the Scriptures other than one page of the Bible in a language foreign to them. When Mark and his friends went from door to door handing out New Testaments in the Albanian language, some people burst into tears. They had never had such a privilege in all their lives! If Christians in countries such as this cannot get a Bible in their own language, how much less likely it would be for a non-Christian to obtain one.

Not everyone can watch Christian broadcasts

No doubt television is a powerful communicator of the Gospel. Millions are being ministered to through this modern mass-communicator, and many are being saved and healed as a result. Yet as gratifying as all this is, one cannot escape certain realities.

In a rare cooperative agreement in 1984, both evangelists and critics commissioned an extensive study by the University of Pennsylvania's Annenberg School of Communications and the Gallup organization. Their purpose: to determine the impact of the Gospel via the medium of television. According to *Time* magazine, the survey revealed that only 6.2% of the American TV audience were regular viewers of the various Christian shows. A 1985 survey by Nielsen added cable data to the statistics. This survey still showed that those households tuning in to gospel television programs for even a few minutes a week were in the minority. [2]

We cannot expect everyone to be reached through this medium. Let us rejoice at everything God is doing through television, but Christian television does not absolve us from the responsibility we each have of personally sharing Christ with those around us.

Another limitation of television is this: Many people in our world do not have a television set. The latest statistics I have read on China state that only a small percentage of homes in that vast land—where one fourth of our planet lives—have a TV set to watch. Millions in that nation alone, to say nothing of huge areas elsewhere on the globe—like the Indian Subcontinent; the tribal regions throughout the earth; and many parts of Africa, Oceania, and Latin America—will never tune in to these gospel broadcasts. They simply don't have the sets and they may never have them.

On top of this, people living in religiously oppressed lands are often denied the privilege of such things as city-wide evangelistic rallies, mass literature crusades, and Christian television and radio programs. But even where access to the Christian media is denied, the Gospel continues to go forth. One example is the way fellow believers were able to win others to Christ all over the former Soviet Empire—sometimes at an astonishing rate.

We have only to consider the early Church to see another example. Of course, their era was before the advent of the printing press, radio, or television. Yet they turned the world upside down! The Gospel wields phenomenal power when simply presented in a Christlike manner by flesh and blood.

Personal evangelism will get the job done faster

Scholars estimate the world's population stood at 500 million in the year 1650. It then took until 1850 to double to one billion. By 1997, the population could easily total six billion. These rapidly increasing masses of people are not going to be reached by just a few hundred or even a few thousand evangelists and ministers. Perhaps the following excerpt will help bring this truth home to us all. Brother Andrew wrote this many years ago, but it should still make us stop and think.

> If no more people were born in China, and if from now on a revival like that on the day of Pentecost took place with 3,000 conversions every day, it would take 725 years before everyone in China was converted. Moreover, 3,000 conversions a day is not very many considering that the population increases by 54,794 every day. [3]

China represents about one-quarter of the world's population. This should prompt the serious question: "How can all the world hear the Gospel so Jesus can return?" This question must be faced, for Matthew 24:14 reads, "And this Gospel of the kingdom will be preached in the whole world as a testimony to all nations, and then the end will come." We know that Christians can actually hasten the day of the Lord from what the apostle Peter wrote: "You ought to live holy and godly lives as you look forward to the day of God and *speed its coming*" (II Peter 3:11-12, italics mine).

We can bring back the King, but every Christian needs to be involved. To see just how possible it is to spread the message of Jesus rapidly, let's for a moment consider that the born-again population of the world numbers only 200 million. That's an absurdly conservative estimate, but it will only serve to strengthen the following illustration.

Let's suppose that every one of these born-again believers leads one other person to Christ each year. Let's also assume that the new convert, in turn, leads someone else to Christ the following year. At this extremely slow rate of growth, the entire world would be Christian in approximately 13 years.

Think of that! If you find this difficult to accept, try working it out with pen and paper. It should be encouraging. One thing that this arithmetical assignment doesn't take into account, however, is the uneven distribution of Christians throughout the world. But even so, the exercise should give us a clear vision of just how possible Jesus' words are to fulfill when He commanded us to preach the Gospel to every creature. (Mark 16:15). Remember,

Jesus' injunction for us to tell everyone about Him was His last emphatic commandment, not His last timid suggestion.

Personal evangelism is vital to a well-balanced Christian life

When I was a teenager, prayer and Bible reading were not exciting to me. Then for some months as I approached my fifteenth birthday, I began asking God to help me be a Christian influence among my classmates at high school.

One day, the opportunity arose after a class discussion on the value of religion throughout history. After the teacher dismissed us, a fellow student with anti-religious sentiments continued to loudly air his views to a few of us as we walked down the corridor. Here was an opportunity. Should I say something?

Once outside the school building, I stopped walking and began to address my friend. But I hardly knew what to say. When I did open my mouth to say something, I was at a loss for meaningful words. Witnessing was something I hardly knew a thing about.

I said what I could (which wasn't much), then felt impeded. About that time, another thought popped into my head. *Why not take him to another Christian who'd know what to say?* So I put the proposal to him, and to my surprise, he accepted. I worked out the details with my brother Max, who was staying in a house with young men from our church. The afternoon arrived, and I introduced my classmate to my brother and the other young men. One of the young men took my friend aside to speak with him, and to my amazement, that classmate ended up coming to Christ!

And the result of this? My prayer and Bible reading after that were never the same. I was fired up, and arose early each morning to seek the Lord. I felt responsible to disciple my school friend, and to see others in my class come to know the Lord, as well.

You see, prayer becomes far more meaningful and specific when we are involved in the real world of people, their needs, and winning them for Christ. And what an encouragement to our prayer life when there are a number of young converts that we as a group or church have led to the Lord. That did not happen to me as a teenager, but it did occur later.

What a thrilling thing to see God answer prayer and deepen the lives of young converts! At the same time, the Bible is much more real when we're reaching out to others as the disciples of Jesus did.

God wants personal evangelism restored to all of the Church

We all know how successful the early Church was in personal evangelism as they scattered over a large area, busily witnessing for Christ. From the Middle East, they took the message up into Europe, down into Africa, and east into Arabia. Though some of them were killed by the sword, beheaded, and thrown to the lions, the Church continued to witness. And travel. By 300 A.D., Christianity had reached the outer extremities of the Roman Empire, which stretched from the border of Scotland to modern-day Kuwait. And still the message traveled. Tradition says that one of the Lord's disciples, Thomas, was martyred in Madras, South India.

Unfortunately, Christianity later became acceptable, and the Church became more concerned with conferences than it was with reaching the regions beyond. Finally, she sank even further during the Dark Ages. Few were born again. The clergy kept the Bible to themselves. Witnessing came pretty much to a standstill. According to one author, clusters of Christians unconnected with the local church kept Christianity alive for hundreds of years. [4]

Many times, an aspect of truth becomes almost extinct to Christians, not because the Bible is silent on that subject, but because so few are living out that facet of God's Word. The path back from medieval times to the Church operating as the Lord Jesus desired has been slow, but steady.

The Body of Christ, however, still needs to be possessed by a passion for witnessing on the personal level. If we evangelize personally with the right motive, others will be drawn to follow our example. Personal evangelism must be restored to the Church all over the world. Will you receive the torch, which is beginning to blaze strongly, then pass it on to others?

2

How Do We Convey Our Message?

Recent research in the business world has indicated that after a salesman has left a client, it is the manner of the salesman's approach that is remembered more than anything else—even more than the content of the salesman's words. The same applies in the world of witnessing. Long after the Christian has left, the unsaved man will remember the manner of the Christian's presentation.

Sometimes, people have not responded positively to my message because I used the wrong approach. It wasn't what I said, but how I said it. Unfortunately, because of past attitudes of "defending the truth," I turned people away from the One I wanted them to know! I have come to the conclusion that we have to represent Christ's goodness to be credible in the world's eyes. Otherwise, they will tune us out.

Actually, outsiders usually see God more readily by our genuine love and concern than by spelling out our beliefs—as important as right doctrine might be. In the many evangelistic outreaches I have led, I've noticed it is not always the Bible college graduate with the correct words who wins more people to Christ. It is the person with the more caring lifestyle. It is the one with the ability to spend time with others because he enjoys them, and they, in turn, know that. Let's consider the "do's" and "don'ts" that we should observe when we speak of Christ.

We should witness naturally

At one point, I was afraid to witness to people. In fact, there were certain individuals I was actually terrified to say anything to. But I have found over the years that the greatest motivator to witness is love. The more love I have for the unsaved, the more natural I feel.

Love is not threatening. When people are convinced we love and care for them, it's amazing how often they will respond correctly to us. That's not to say that it will always work like that. We have to be prepared for our words to be opposed or politely ignored.

I have also found that the more I witness, the easier it becomes. If I don't witness for a while, the fear of man comes creeping back. But it's never as bad as it used to be. The experience of the fullness of the Holy Spirit and His love, plus the confidence I have learned from witnessing in the past, can all be resummoned.

We must be friendly

We all know that God strongly desires friendship with us. That is why He made man in the beginning. Although man's sin deeply grieved God, He wanted fellowship with His creatures to be restored. Accordingly, He actively began wooing man back to Himself. A God of lesser character would have rejected us. But not our God. He loves man.

To help us be more friendly as we witness, it's good to remember that salvation is knowing and loving God (John 17:3). So when we witness, our job is to encourage people to know and love Him.

The best way I know to do that is to explain the character of God. People will not be inspired to know someone they're afraid of. They will, however, be drawn to someone whose personality captivates them.

Jesus said, "When I am lifted up from the earth, [I] will draw all men to myself" (John 12:32). The immediate interpretation of being "lifted up" is the Crucifixion. But it has a wider meaning, as well. Calvary was an exhibition to the universe of Christ's determination to love sinners and to provide a way of forgiveness for those who are penitent. We must reinforce this concept by enjoying being friendly with people.

Jesus did. As holy as He was, gamblers, prostitutes, and cheaters felt loved, understood, and even honored by Him. (Luke 19:5; John 4:9,28-30). By loving sinners and spending time in their company, He gave them a chance to change their ways (Luke

19:8-9, John 4:41-42). So must we. Some might ask, "Well, if Jesus' character will draw people to Himself, why doesn't everyone get saved?" The reason, of course, is that people can dig in their heels and resist. Sadly, many do, just as Jesus explained in Matthew 7:13.

But even if sinners have no intention of turning to God, we must still continue to love them (Mark 10:21). For too long, we Christians have been guilty of "loving" people for what we can get out of them—a signed decision card or a warm body in a pew.

The only people to whom Jesus spoke sharply were hypocritical spiritual leaders, or those who had been exposed to a lot of truth (Matthew 23). That's because much is required of those to whom much is given (Luke 12:48). Most people we talk to may never have understood the Gospel—especially those brought up in a secular environment or a non-Christian culture. Let's be patient with them. Remember, we also were in darkness once, and during those years, we justified our sinful actions.

We should be good listeners

I remember setting out one summer on a Greyhound bus from Los Angeles to Northern California. Before I even got on board, I asked the Lord to place me beside someone He wanted me to witness to. Well, that trip was fairly uneventful to begin with. But about halfway through the journey, I heard raised voices in the rear of the bus.

Turning to see what was going on, I noticed an older lady coming up the aisle toward me, cursing and muttering to herself. She plunked her large frame into the empty place next to me. I glanced at her scowling face as she settled into the seat, and thought how bitter she looked. I remember thinking, *Someone in her life has really hurt her.*

Before long, we were engaged in deep conversation. At one point, she spat out, "I've buried one husband and divorced the other!" Evidently, both had been alcoholics. In fact, the disruption in the back of the bus had been her reaction to a drunkard whose actions had triggered memories of the past. Unfortunately, she had allowed her hurt to turn into bitterness.

She continued to talk, and I listened. Suddenly she stopped and asked, "Why am I telling you all this?" After a pause, she said, "I know. It's because people today don't listen!" After that, I began to notice something rather remarkable. Those hard lines on her face had softened. I was now sitting beside a very likeable old lady. Sympathetic listening had done wonders for her!

If you have a desire to listen, you will grow in compassion. And with compassion, you'll inspire people to open up to you. As a general rule, it's good to let a person say what he or she wants to—within reason. To interrupt can make him feel that we don't care, and that will work against us.

Listening sympathetically is the opposite of arguing. We are not listening when we argue, because we are so intent on getting our view across. Arguing demeans. It says: "My view and I are more important than what you think. I don't respect your opinion, and so I don't respect you." When that happens, the other person's perception of us is that we are arrogant. But if we listen, his perception is that we really do respect him. Sinners need to feel that we think they're important, that they have value, and that they are irreplaceable. That's exactly how God looks upon them.

In a book written many years ago, Dorothy Walter Baruch mentioned the things everybody needs in order to function in emotional strength, regardless of age. The two most important needs, she wrote, are acceptance and understanding. "We need desperately to be able to share our thoughts and feelings with some one person...who really understands." [5] People will feel accepted when we listen sympathetically.

We must use simple terms when we witness

Each profession uses words and expressions almost unintelligible to members of a different occupation. You only have to overhear the conversation of two doctors (or two computer experts) to be convinced of this.

Unfortunately, we Christians sound just the same to non-Christians when we use our special terms. The importance of speaking to people in terms they can understand cannot be overemphasized.

We waste many hours because we do not clarify the terms we use. Just consider the following true story: One young man in America, who was not familiar with "Christianese," read a sign which announced, "Jesus saves." He honestly thought it meant that Jesus was thrifty with His money!

The chances are that if we use terms like *personal Savior, redeemed, born again, or justified,* we will not be getting through to our non-churchgoing friends. When we speak, we should never give our listeners that "left-out" feeling. That's the feeling you get when the doctor explains you have *dyshidrosis* or uses some other medical term. Instead of saying *repentance,* we can talk about turning from everything we know is wrong. Instead of *justification*, we could talk about forgiveness.

Many of us think that it's automatic that God's Word will not return to Him void (Isaiah 55:11). Scripture must balance Scripture, however, for Jesus taught that if a man does not understand the message of the Gospel, then the devil removes those very words that we have spoken (Matthew 13:19). God is the greatest communicator, and He speaks in ways that others clearly understand. Only when His message is sent in His way and His timing will it be understood and "not return to Him void." Our goal is to present our message as clearly as God does—in a simple, dynamic way.

We should witness for Christ with enthusiasm

This is sometimes more easily said than done. While it is true that witnessing brings its own joy, there are times when we feel anything but enthusiastic about witnessing.

This is where faith needs to be exercised. I believe faith is simply doing what God has told us to do, with the right attitude of heart. We must remind ourselves that when we witness, we are sharing the message which God gave to mankind at great cost. We are also obeying the words of Jesus Christ, who commanded us to speak forth for Him (Mark 16:15). But we also have to bear in mind that if we don't exhibit a Christlike life, we communicate nothing.

Remember, witnessing is spiritual warfare. The devil does well to attack our feelings, because so many of us are influenced by them. But if we do not let our feelings rule us, he'll have a hard time derailing our witnessing efforts. So what can we do to keep from letting feelings drag us down?

The Scriptures tell us: "Submit yourselves, then, to God. Resist the devil, and he will *flee* from you. Come near to God and he will come near to you" (James 4:7, italics mine). According to this verse, the devil will not flee if we are not submitted to the Lord.

In Hebrews 13:15-16 we are exhorted to take a further step. Part of that passage reads, "Let us continually offer to God a sacrifice of praise." This includes praising God for who He is, not for how we may feel. The devil does not hang around thankful people—nor do feelings of self-pity. Many of us fail God at this point, because the moment the devil gets upset and attacks us with depression and discouragement, we tend to slow down our work for the Lord.

A note of caution. God never approves of falsehood and pretense. If we know we have unconfessed sin, trying to maintain a positive attitude and to rejoice in the Lord doesn't work very well. If we are aware of sin in our lives, we need to confess it and forsake it. After all, we can't very well tell non-Christians to do something we are not doing.

If we're not aware of anything wrong in our lives, we need to be like David in I Samuel 30:6: "David encouraged himself in the Lord his God."

For example, on a door-to-door witnessing outreach in Canada some years ago, two young Christians received a rude reception from a lady whose door they had approached. They encouraged themselves that God was the same, regardless of how people received them.

Still rejoicing, they made their way back down the path while the woman watched from the window. She was struck by their joyful attitudes. When they had worked their way from house to house down the street and back up the other side, she beckoned them over. Somewhat taken aback, the young Christians crossed the road. This time, the woman's attitude was altogether different, and she invited them into her home. After hearing their message, she asked Jesus into her life!

What attracted her to the Lord? I believe it was the reality of God in their lives, manifested by their joyful attitude. The Gospel must be alive in us, not just words printed in a book.

This is not to say that doctrine is unimportant. In fact, some people are drawn to God by hearing or reading truth, like Nicodemus (John 3). But for many others, like the woman in the previous example, seeing Christians with the joy of the Lord in the face of rejection will speak louder than words. As Stephen was being stoned to death (Acts 7:54-8:1), who knows how much the peace on his face ministered to hard-hearted Saul of Tarsus, the persecutor of the Church?

The Christian walks a unique pathway because he is linked with God and has the same power behind him that brought creation into being. Unlike the founders of every other religion, the founder of the Christian faith has risen from the dead. When we witness, we must remember that the resurrection power of Christ is available to us. It is no credit to Him if we witness reluctantly. The will of God for us is to rejoice in the Lord always, and to make melody in our hearts to the Lord (Colossians 3:16, Philippians 4:4).

3

The Necessity of Prayer

Years ago, Margaret and I were with a team witnessing daily in a suburb of Bangkok, Thailand. Each afternoon, we set out in pairs with literature in hand to witness to anyone willing to talk with us. At least that was the plan. Doing it was another matter, for the going was tough in this Buddhist stronghold. But we kept going, and as we shared the Gospel, we invited people to attend the three evening meetings scheduled for later in the week.

When time for the first meeting arrived, we were disappointed at the poor attendance. What should we do? We made the decision to pray the next day instead of witnessing. We prayed for hours, then went expectantly to the meeting. But we were disappointed again. The attendance was no better—it was even worse!

The next day, we resumed our witnessing schedule, and we immediately sensed a difference. We felt we were getting somewhere as we witnessed. That night, more people came to the meeting, and we felt more of the presence of God. It was a graphic lesson to us: *we must have a heart to both pray and witness—the two go together.*

Several months later, we arrived in the southern Philippine city of Davao where we were to stay for some time, working with a church and teaching the members about evangelism. We went witnessing daily, sometimes taking people from the church with us. We were invited many times to preach at different classes in a nearby college.

One day early in our stay in Davao, Margaret was impressed in her daily Bible reading with a verse from Isaiah which read, "You who call on the Lord, give yourselves no rest, and give *him* no rest till he establishes Jerusalem" (Isaiah 62:6-7, italics mine).

Inspired by that verse, we decided to do something bold: For two months, the eight of us on that team maintained an around-the-clock prayer vigil praying for Davao, for our ministry of witnessing and preaching, and for the contacts we had begun to make. After a few weeks, we started to see things happen.

The first person to make a move toward God was a college student named Helen. She gave her heart to the Lord about the third week of our prayer vigil. One of our team members met with Helen most afternoons after classes, and the two of them prayed, studied the Word of God, and went witnessing together.

For a month, just the two of them met together, but soon a small group of Helen's friends joined their afternoon meetings. One day, one of Helen's teachers was feeling so sick that she asked Helen to pray for her. Her fever left instantly! What a joy Helen has been to us down through the years. Today she looks back on about fourteen years of full-time Christian service.

Another day during our time in Davao, I talked with a young college student named Jackson. He was committed totally to the philosophy of communism, and so he disagreed with our teaching. As we talked, a thought occurred to me, and I shared it with him.

"Jackson, suppose we were to take all the wealth of the Philippines and pile it in a heap here on the street, and then divide it equally with everyone in the country. Would that solve all the woes of this nation which were caused by corruption?" He looked at me, but said nothing. A little later, he excused himself and took his leave.

The next time I saw Jackson, he told me that he had wrestled with my question until 2:00 a.m. He decided that only Christ could solve the nation's troubles, and had given his life to the Lord. Today he pastors the very church where we talked 21 years ago!

Others who came to Christ as a result of all that praying and witnessing are still going on for the Lord today. They have been a joy to us over the years.

People in some parts of the world, like the Philippines, are much more sensitive to the reality of the spiritual world. So when you go in and hold a Gospel meeting, it's easy to draw large crowds and see many respond to the altar call. But lasting conversions and changed lives are a different matter.

As I look back on what took place in Davao all those years ago, I see another valuable lesson: *Concerted effort in prayer leads to remarkable conversions that last the test of time.*

It's obvious that Jesus understood this principle, because He spent long hours in prayer. One time, He dismissed the crowds to be alone in prayer until the early morning hours (Matthew 14:23-25). The next day, He operated in power and healed "all who touched him" (verse 36). Other passages record Jesus' many hours of prayer in a solitary place either long before daybreak or during the night hours (Mark 1:35; Luke 5:16; 6:12). If it was necessary for the Son of God to pray like this to be fruitful and effective in His ministry, we should follow His example, or do more!

Anyone who wants to win people to the Lord needs to learn about a phenomenon called revival. That's a term often given to a move of God when thousands are converted, and society is affected and changed as a result. If you study revivals in Church history, you'll see that travailing prayer precedes revival.

Perhaps the most widely known revival was the Welsh revival of 1904. Evan Roberts, a 26-year-old man who was studying for the ministry, had been praying for 13 months for the Holy Spirit to sweep his land. Other intercessors were also praying when revival broke out in Wales, but Evan had been praying so hard and had spent so many hours praying and preaching in his bedroom that his landlady became afraid and asked him to leave! During the Welsh revival, 100,000 people obeyed God in repentance and entered the Kingdom of God in a short space of time. [6]

Are you convinced that you should pray? If so, where do you start? I think we should begin by ensuring that we have adequate time each day with God in what is often called a "quiet time." This is regular time spent alone in prayer with God. Having a quiet time each day is like giving our money away in offerings. We don't give offerings to the Lord because we have a lot of extra money, but because we want to give to the Lord, and we see that it is right. We also believe that God will help us get through the month financially. That's all part of the walk of faith.

It's the same with our time aside with God each day. Most of us can't "afford" that time before we start a busy day (or before we flop into bed at night). But we do it anyway, out of love for God. We also believe that God will help us find the time to do those things that are really necessary.

Once we have a regular quiet time established, we can think of some extra times to spend in prayer. Some suggestions for these extra times are: while standing at a bus stop, while waiting in a car for the traffic lights to change, or while waiting "forever" for our turn at the doctor's office!

The ancient Jews used to pray three times a day: at dawn, at noon, and again at sunset (Psalm 55:17; Daniel 6:10). Perhaps that's why the apostle Peter went up on the roof at noon to pray in Acts 10:9. But it may also have been because he'd just found out that he had a few minutes to spare before lunch. In any event, he spent that time in prayer, and God gave him a great revelation. The result was the very first Gentile group of people coming to Christ (Acts 10).

Obviously, our personal communion with the Lord is of the utmost importance, and takes priority over all other forms of prayer. After all, salvation is knowing and walking with God (John 17:3). But prayer also includes concern that others would come to know the Lord. We should pray that God will help us to be better witnesses for Him.

We can witness for Christ whether we witness one on one, have a partner with us, or go in a group. But for the sake of consistency in our presentation, let's assume that you'll usually have a witnessing partner.

Pray with your partner before you set out to witness. Begin by quieting your hearts before God, then offer your witnessing time as a gift of love for God to use as He sees fit. Believe God will lead you to the right people—those whose attention has never before been on spiritual matters, and those ready to obey the Lord, repent, and begin a love relationship with God.

With each encounter, one should pray while the other talks. The job of the praying partner is not to listen and throw in a thought now and then. Your prayers can affect the conversation powerfully.

The success of this encounter may depend upon your prayers.

Pray against distractions like crying children and ringing telephones. Things like this can distract the person we're witnessing to, and keep him from understanding our message. Pray that the Holy Spirit will convince him of God's tender love, and His desire to enter into loving fellowship with him. Sometimes you may need to pray against Satan, who has blinded people to the truths of the Gospel (II Corinthians 4:4).

But our praying should not stop when the conversation ends. Take some time with your partner immediately following a good time of witnessing to pray specifically for that person. The Holy Spirit has words to use—words you have spoken. He will remind the person of your example of godliness, joy, and peace—the fragrance of Christ demonstrated in your life.

Unfortunately, our reasons for praying for the unsaved can be rather selfish. We may pray that our evangelistic outreach or our church be considered very "successful." Or we may pray for people to be saved because it will make life easier for us—especially if they are our friends or relatives.

We must understand that God doesn't answer prayers for someone's salvation which are uttered in anger. God loves people, and unless we pray lovingly for someone, I don't believe that much will happen. In her excellent booklet *How to Pray for Someone Near You Who is Away from God,* Joy Dawson points this out very clearly. She says that when it comes to praying for your relatives, you're praying for people who may have hurt you deeply. "Because of this, we need to make sure there is no resentment in our hearts toward them as we pray." [7]

Joy tells the story of a lady in California who had an unsaved son-in-law. For years he had been cruel to the lady's daughter and her grandchildren. His family suffered greatly as a result. All this time, this fine Christian lady prayed fervently, but without result.

One night, she heard Joy speak about the importance of forgiving those who have hurt you. She was convicted of her resentment toward her unsaved son-in-law, so she diligently jotted down Joy's eight-point message on practical steps to overcome resentment.

Once she got home, she fell on her knees and repented of her resentment. She put those eight points into practice, one by one. That was at 11:30 p.m. on a Thursday evening.

On the following Saturday morning, the lady was startled as her son-in-law burst into her home. This was totally unexpected, since he lived several hours' drive away. He explained that at exactly 11:30 p.m. on Thursday night, he had come under heavy conviction of sin, and had repented and had given his life to Christ! He had asked his wife and children to forgive him, and now felt compelled to ask forgiveness from his mother-in-law.

So another valuable lesson to learn in praying for people to come to know Christ is to pray in love.

Another important aspect of prayer for conversions is that Christians should be brokenhearted over their own sins. This is particularly true if they want to see revival.

At the beginning of his reign as king of Israel, Solomon asked God for wisdom. God answered by explaining that if there is a drought or any other calamity, the people of God should do something about it. In other words, it was not labor unions, radicals, or governments who should pray and humble themselves. It was God's people who were required to do that (II Chronicles 7:13-14).

It is the same with us today. My paraphrase of I Peter 4:17 goes like this: "Conviction of sin must start in the house of God before we can expect it to occur among outsiders." As Christians, we have to turn from everything we know to be wrong before we can expect sinners to be affected.

In 1949, Christians in the Scottish Hebrides cried out to God for the removal of the spiritual drought on their land. Twice a week, people met in an old barn and prayed through the night. But it was not until they began confessing their sin that God moved in power. Because the Christians had humbled themselves first, the Lord was justly able to send His conviction upon the unsaved.

The conviction of sin was felt so strongly in the area that one night young people fled from a dance hall at 2:00 a.m. to seek God in a neighboring church. Even drunkards called out to God for mercy in the street. This move of God in the Hebrides saw thousands swept into His Kingdom in a matter of months.

We must also understand that we may be playing a role in keeping someone from coming to Christ. We may have committed a sin (whether before or after our own salvation) which is a stumbling block to that person. If so, we must go to that person—relative, friend, classmate, fellow employee, or former employer—and humble ourselves by asking for forgiveness.

We are only as effective in evangelism as we are effective in prayer. Besides the other reasons just listed, prayer is fellowship with God. That's where we get to know Him. If we don't know Him very well, we won't be able to share with others about Him very effectively.

We can only share God's love and presence to the extent that we know it in our own lives. A hurting world needs to see what God is like. If God is speaking to us in prayer, and we are enjoying friendship with Him, our lives will readily reflect the life of Christ. When a sinner sees Jesus in us, he will respond much more quickly to what we say. If we know God, the natural result will be that we will make Him known to others. To be effective, we must grow to know God more and more.

When we discuss the subject of follow-up later in this book, we will again address the importance of prayer, because the apostle Paul prayed constantly for those he preached to and labored among (Ephesians 1:16-18; I Thessalonians 1:2-3; II Timothy 1:3-4).

4

Sharing a Testimony

A powerful part of our "witnessing toolbox" is sharing our testimony. As we tell others about Christ, we will meet those who refuse to recognize the truths we present. Don't get discouraged: Your testimony is vital and powerful. How can anyone deny what has actually happened to you? They can't. That's why it has such authority. A person with an experience is never at the mercy of someone who merely has an argument. Following are some guidelines for sharing our testimonies with an unbelieving world.

Always speak from a "low" position

We should never "preach" when we give our testimony. We should avoid giving the appearance of being "high and mighty" because of what has happened to us. Remember, we must be Christlike, and never give a cynical world the opportunity of saying that we are arrogant. We must convey both warmth and the understanding that what we've experienced, they can, too.

Be relevant

As you consider how best to communicate the character of God to the person you're witnessing to, choose the slice of your testimony which he can best relate to and understand. If, for example, I'm talking to someone who has a problem with anger, I can get his attention easily when I explain how I used to fight with my brothers before my conversion. But I can also lose the attention of easygoing people by using that same illustration. Some people warm up to me when I tell them how Billy Graham played a part in my conversion; others turn off completely when they hear that. The rule of thumb should be to ask yourself: "What would appeal to me if I were in that person's shoes?"

Be specific

If we speak in general terms, saying things like, "There's been a wonderful change in my life," it's going to mean very little to the other person. But when we deliberately pinpoint exactly what the Lord has transformed in our lives, it will have a greater impact. We need to mention those things from which we have been delivered, like anxiety, boredom, addiction, and guilt. These are real problems in many people's lives today, and our listener will easily grasp what we're talking about if they identify with us.

While listening to one particular speaker, I noticed that the audience became most attentive when he told about his battle with worry. He had been filled with fear while traveling as a fix-it man for a large corporation. Not only was he afraid of flying, but he was plagued with anxiety that he wouldn't be able to do what was required of him. The night before such a business trip, he tossed and turned despite the comfort of his hotel bed. Because the speaker was so specific about his problem and how he had conquered it through Christ, he had our complete attention.

As we share things like this, people will realize that God can change their lives in those specific areas, too. The power of our testimony resides in the fact that we've triumphed over a weakness. That makes others sit up and take notice.

Christianity is an inward change of heart. I believe it does more good if we tell others how Christ has turned us from selfishness and covetousness, and has helped us to overcome feelings of revenge, lust, or pride than to tell them about the outward differences—like the fact we don't drink, smoke, or party any more.

Be truthful

If we've gained our listener's attention by testifying about victory over a particular sin, they may ask about other things, as well. What happens if they question us about an area in which we still have battles?

Good question. If Christians have obvious sin in their lives, they shouldn't be witnessing at all. But what if they still worry, get angry occasionally, or battle with resentment?

Think of it from your listener's point of view. If you were seeking God, who would you listen to? Someone who says he doesn't have any problems? Or someone who admits he still has a worry or two? Who would seem more believable?

Jesus taught that the Holy Spirit is the spirit of truth (John 16:13). The endorsement of the Holy Spirit—which is absolutely essential if our witness is to be effective—cannot come upon our words unless what we say is true. Some of us might be tempted to think, *If I exaggerate just a little, my testimony will sound more impressive*. Don't do it! When what we say is untrue, the Holy Spirit can't back our words.

Don't confine your testimony to your salvation experience

To prove how real and personal God is to us, we should share our stories of God's protection, provision, and care for us since our conversion. In many ways, this gives the sinner a more rounded picture of what being a Christian will involve, and may well be the point of attraction to Christ.

When we share God's truth in a testimony, it appeals to people better than telling about a doctrinal position. People have said to me often that they love listening to my stories. What are they referring to? When I share a segment of my life that illustrates the truth I am trying to convey, they see that God is real. They can know Him and trust Him.

Give up-to-date testimonies

We must spend daily time with the Lord, and daily overcome temptations in our lives before we can witness effectively. Let's not just tell how Christ has changed our lives or has spoken to us in recent years. Let's also share how He is changing our lives and speaking to us today.

I have found that if I can tell about something that has happened in my life in the last week (in my quiet time, in my ministry to others, or in terms of guidance and so on), it is my most effective communication. Don't be afraid to be perfectly natural. After all, people confer with fortune tellers and look up the horoscopes in magazines because they are looking for guidance and comfort. Why shouldn't they consider consulting the God of all the universe, and consider following Him for the rest of their lives?

In the same way as the testimony of a witness in a court case can sway the jury in their decision to either convict or free someone from blame, the power of our testimony helps people make a decision about Christ. Don't be discouraged if you don't end up leading a certain person to Christ. Later on, that individual may look back on your testimony as the vital one that helped influence him to make the right choice. If so, it will be a choice that he'll thank God for throughout all eternity!

5

How to Open the Conversation

We come now to a vital question: "How on earth do we change an everyday conversation to a spiritual one?"

Some Christians never attempt to change the direction of an ordinary conversation at all. They only witness when someone asks them specifically about their faith. Many of us are either in that category or have been.

Other Christians use the approach of "taking the bull by the horns." They tell someone that they want to talk about Christian things and ask a leading question such as, "What do you think of God?" or "Have you ever thought about becoming a Christian?"

Many who use this approach insist that it's the only way to witness. "Otherwise, we're not being honest," they tell me, "and non-Christians are not going to appreciate it any other way." Some who favor this position feel that it's good to get a conversation rolling by bringing up a topical issue like abortion or gay rights, and use that as a springboard for witnessing.

In between these two positions are those who feel they should witness more often than just when they are asked about their faith, but they feel more comfortable about waiting for an appropriate topic of conversation to come up naturally, then steer that into a conversation about the Lord. Which way is right?

Your decision on which approach to use will depend in part on what you feel comfortable with, unless you feel a conviction from the Lord that you are to use another method. Although I have used all three options, the middle-of-the-road method is one I seem to enjoy using, as the following incidents illustrate.

Late one Sunday night, I decided to call a friend long-distance. The operator placed the call, but no one answered the phone. When the operator came back on the line, she said that my friend must be at a party. I could easily have thanked her and hung up, but I sensed an opportunity to witness, so I decided to continue the conversation.

"No, she won't be at a party. She's probably at church." I knew this should stir some interest, because it was so late that most people would have left church hours earlier.

"At church! What church?" the operator asked, incredulous.

I told her the name of my friend's church, then asked casually, "Are you interested in Christian things?"

Her reply was not very positive, so I asked why she felt that way. Our conversation lasted for 15 minutes, and I finally had to end it. But I got the operator's address so I could send her some literature. I also invited her to talk further with Margaret and me over dinner. She didn't accept, but that shows how well the conversation had gone, for me to even suggest a get-together. And because she was an operator on duty, she could have cut me off at any point. But she obviously had become interested in our discussion.

In this example, the telephone operator opened the door by asking, "At church! What church?" She didn't ask me how to get saved, but she did question me about something to do with Christianity. I answered her question, then as naturally as possible, kept the general topic of Christianity alive by moving it into a more serious theme—was she interested in spiritual things?

The "direct question" or the "reference to spiritual matters" approach is an upfront one. It might simply be a comment on an everyday topic that paves the way for you to naturally guide the conversation to spiritual matters.

For example, I was in the inner city of Auckland, New Zealand, about to collect my shoes from a repairman. Upon entering the store, the cheerful repairman, complete with apron around his waist, greeted me. As he gave me my newly repaired shoes, he looked at them for a moment, then made a "door-opening" comment to me.

"I'm not likely to see you again," he said brightly. "I've done such a good job on these shoes that they'll need no further repair!"

Hmm, I thought, *here's an opportunity to say something.* Little did he know that I was in charge of a witnessing program in which young people went from house to house for a week at a time.

In a natural way, I told him how much walking I did, and explained why. Then I asked, "Are you interested in these things?"

We chatted back and forth as he tore a length of brown paper from a big roll attached to the counter and began wrapping my shoes. Another customer came in, but it seemed to make no difference to the repairman.

By this time, I'd paid for the shoes and the wrapping process had finished, but he kept talking, then listening to what I had to say. Finally, I felt so sorry for the other customer that I ended the conversation. But I did continue the next time I came into the shop.

The way you open the conversation will depend upon the temperament of the person you are approaching. I do a lot of witnessing on airplanes, and if I feel the person beside me does not have an outgoing personality, I leave him alone for perhaps half the flight or more. When I do begin to open up a conversation, he is more likely to enter into a time of talking, because I have respected his privacy for a decent length of time. They usually reward me by willingly entering into a meaningful time of conversation.

It is important to respect a person's culture, too. Many Americans want to know up front what you want to talk about. If this is the type of person you are dealing with, it would be to your advantage to fit into his framework.

But in many cultures, the opposite is true. They are offended if you immediately state what's on your mind. Businessmen who travel to the Middle East know that you should never start negotiations until your client feels that he knows you well enough to trust you. Actually, most of the world thinks like that. In these cultures, those times you spend getting to know one another over coffee are "money in the bank" to the businessman wanting to strike a deal. In the realm of witnessing, it's the same thing.

Whichever way you choose to open a conversation, I must stress the need for you to be natural, not blunt. It's important to avoid times of awkward silences or strained conversations whenever possible.

People will listen if our approach is friendly. In those countries where attitudes and religions have prejudiced people against our Lord Jesus, it is even more important to use a more indirect and friendly approach. If we feel embarrassed, they will, too. But if we feel friendly and natural, they will feel at ease. After all, Christianity is the norm, as far as God is concerned. Why shouldn't we feel confident?

A major key in opening a conversation—and indeed a major key to witnessing in general—is to *always start off in an area of agreement.* If you start off with an area of contention, you're fighting a losing battle. You've set the tone for the whole conversation. Instead, you want to get your friend pulling and agreeing with you.

Before you start to testify, it can be helpful if you can find some common ground—the same occupation or interest in life. That's not always possible, so you may need to look for some other means of connecting. Sometimes you can identify with them in other ways. You may know what it is to lose a loved one, to be laid off work, or to have wrecked the family car. Your means of identification may be that you have been to their home town or know a mutual friend. We need to put our friends at ease so that they can relate to us.

When I witness, I often am asked about my occupation. At one time, I usually replied that I was a missionary. *Why not be bold and upfront?* I used to think. That's the way to start witnessing. While that approach started a few conversations, I noticed that many other people suddenly cooled toward me. My attempt to start a conversation often backfired because a wall would come between us.

Now I try to ease into conversations about Christianity, rather than jerk people into them. When I'm asked about my occupation, I might say that I am a lecturer. As the conversation progresses, I might mention that I'm connected to a Christian university, and move into a witnessing conversation that way.

On the other hand, when I'm witnessing on the street among the less educated, I often refrain from mentioning the word *university.* In personal evangelism, it is essential to identify with people and make them feel at ease.

We have spent most of this chapter telling how to slip into spiritual conversations—probably because this is what I do a lot. But there's another reason why it has been good to dwell on this approach. That's because the only way I can see all the world hearing the message of Christ is for every Christian to be involved in personal evangelism.

It may be too much to ask most Christians to start witnessing on the streets. But I believe more Christians would become active in personal evangelism if they could learn a more gradual approach. After a while, it becomes quite natural to move from an everyday topic to a spiritual one.

Even if opportunities to witness don't appear by themselves, we can bring them about quite naturally, as we have already seen. But we will not take these opportunities if we do not love the unsaved, or if we are more intent upon living for material comforts than for God.

Despite this chapter's emphasis on gradually opening the conversation, there are times when I witness without a "door" being opened. For example, I have approached someone with the comment, "I don't know what you're going to think of this, but I have an impression that I should talk to you. Do Christian things mean anything to you?"

You may ask, "What about those times of organized witnessing, like being part of some church-sponsored witnessing drive or a Youth With A Mission style outreach? How do we start talking with people during those times?"

In those kinds of situations, we are obviously not making contact with people for any other reason than to preach Christ. Even when we deliberately go out to the streets, the park, or the hospital to witness, we should act naturally, and believe that we have the right to be doing what we are doing. And we should be gentle and friendly in our approach. This will go a long way to endear us to those we are contacting. If we think of some comment about the weather, about the children, or about the surroundings, it is not wrong to offer this. Jesus did. He asked the woman at the well for a drink, and even began talking about water.

When on these special outreaches, it is normal to introduce yourself, the name of your church or organization (if you're in a culture friendly to Christianity), and the most inoffensive reason for doing what you are doing. An introduction like the following is often possible:

"Good morning. My name is John, and this is my friend Jim. We want to tell you something important—how our lives have been completely changed. You see, two years ago, I...." You'll find that kind of approach often very acceptable. And, when going door to door in developing nations, it is usual to be invited inside to talk. Politely and gratefully accept this invitation. People are more likely to respond to you in the privacy of their home.

But in certain environments, you will be inviting a cold reception if you mention Christ or His Church in the first sentence. In these situations, you are wise to follow the biblical pattern and introduce the concept of God first. It took the Godhead at least 4,000 years to prepare humanity for the advent of Christ. In the same way, you need to lay a foundation before introducing Jesus.

In Thailand, we once used a technique which effectively got us involved in conversation with the inhabitants of the housing block where we were witnessing. (This approach will work in a friendly, talkative society. I'd be hesitant to do it in a cynical or critical one. They could quite easily be offended.) The Bangkok missionaries with whom we were working had prepared a list of questions which we presented at each door as part of a religious survey.

Besides asking them their religion (which was usually Buddhist), we asked them their occupation and other relevant details. After recording this information, we asked if they had ever studied any other religion and come to any conclusion about the beginning of the world. Since a pure Buddhist does not believe that God created the world, this approach normally started a conversation.

Let's return to the North American scene. Sometimes when we ask people if they are interested in talking, they will say, "No." At this point, we must be sensitive to the Spirit. Sometimes we should respect that, and perhaps just leave a tract with them, if they care to take one.

At other times, however, you may feel impressed to ask, "Oh, is there some particular reason why you are not interested?" This can lead them into saying why they take exception to the Gospel—an objection to which you may well be able to respond. Actually, they may be very interested in hearing your reply.

Sometimes I have asked in a kind way, "Aren't you interested in a loving God who cares about you?" That question has, at times, kept the conversation going. But we have to be careful not to be obnoxious. God has given people a free will, which means that they have the freedom to say "No, I don't want to listen to you." It is important to know when to be friendly (and sensitively pursue the conversation), and when to back off in a friendly manner.

We should be careful not to force a tract on someone who doesn't want one. It could be that they'll accept a tract from a Christian in the future because we have respected their decision this time. Whatever we do, we should always end the contact in such a way that they will readily welcome another Christian into their lives. Perhaps the next Christian will take them one step closer to the Lord until finally someone will be able to lead them to faith.

On the other hand, I think we occasionally miss opportunities that can lead to conversions. Who knows what may have been the outcome of Melville's life (the banker from Sri Lanka) if I had not asked to see him again?

So now we know how to open the conversation. What do we say after that?

Section II

Presenting the Message

6

A Pattern to Follow

Once we have opened a witnessing conversation with an unsaved friend, what do we say? As we turn to the Word of God, we see that the apostle Paul had two very different approaches, each depending on his audience. We can learn a lot from Paul.

To understand his first approach, let's pretend that we're Jews sitting in a synagogue in Antioch. The rabbi has invited a visiting rabbi to speak, as is customary. We've heard of this rabbi named Saul, but he's now called Paul. His friend Barnabas is with him (as told in Acts 13).

Paul stands on the dais in the center of the synagogue, relating Israeli history and quoting Scriptures about the promised Messiah. We love hearing these cherished words again. But wait? He's saying that this Messiah has already come! Listen to how he's relating the life, death, and resurrection of that miracle-worker called Jesus to the Scriptures he just quoted! This sounds like blasphemy, but it also makes a lot of sense. Paul speaks with such conviction in his voice. Could it be true?

The point of this exercise is to show that although Paul was introducing a new concept to his audience, he did it in a way that the hearer could more readily accept. *He used thoughts with which the hearers were already familiar, then moved logically to new concepts.* When Paul used this approach in Antioch, "the people invited them to speak further about these things on the next Sabbath." The second time, almost the whole city gathered to hear the word of the Lord (Acts 13:42-44).

Let's look at Paul's second approach. This time, he was in Lystra, talking to a completely different kind of audience. The patron god of Lystra was Zeus, the Greek god who was supreme ruler of men. The Greeks had come to regard Zeus as the only god who was concerned with the whole universe. [8]

Even though Lystra was a heathen city, it didn't take long for the apostles to gather a crowd and begin preaching. A man who had never walked listened carefully as Paul spoke. Being sensitive to the Holy Spirit, Paul "saw that he had faith to be healed and called out, 'Stand up on your feet!' " (Acts 14:9-10). At this command, the man jumped up and began to walk. The crowd went wild!

Their enthusiasm was understandable. After all, how often does a miracle like this happen? But their exhilaration was also misguided. The crowd began shouting, "The gods have come down to us in human form!" (verse 11). They started calling Barnabas "Zeus," and they called Paul "Hermes," after the Greek "messenger to the gods." The atmosphere was so charged that it was hard for Paul to even start explaining the Gospel. But when he did, Paul gave a message that holds a lot of importance to us.

The apostle began talking about the concrete concepts of rain from heaven, crops in their seasons, food in abundance, and the emotions of enjoying all these things. In this way, he taught about the existence of a Creator whose character was good (verse 15). By doing this, he again taught new precepts by building upon concepts they already held.

We could call this *the principle of finding common ground.* Although Paul's intended sermon was cut short because of opposition from a third party, enough of his address is recorded for us to know that he started out well. He had forged a link between his thinking and that of his audience, making the Gospel more understandable to them. We should use this kind of approach when talking with those who say they don't believe in God, or with those whose concept of the character of God is distorted—like it certainly was in Lystra.

"Fine," you might say. "I've learned that Paul found common ground among the Jews and the heathen, then moved on from there. But is that really two different approaches?" If you look more closely at these two examples, you'll see something very relevant to us as we evangelize here at home and around the world.

The attitude of the hearer makes the difference. When talking to those familiar with the Scriptures, Paul used that as the basis for his argument. But nowhere in Acts do we find any of the apostles quoting Scripture to those who were not familiar with them.

Although Paul did not actually quote the Bible in Lystra, he preached the truth of the Word of God in terms that the people could relate to. By using illustrations about rain, good crops, and so on, he got the spirit of the Word of God across to them without actually quoting it. After all, there is little point in saying, "Thus saith Moses," when they had no idea who Moses was! And when Paul moved in faith and healed the man who had been lame from birth (Acts 14:8-10), he communicated something of the truth of what God was like.

These two illustrations are not isolated incidents in the book of Acts. The apostle Peter, for example, quoted freely from God's Word on the day of Pentecost (Acts 3:12-26). Again, since the hearers were either Jews or were Jewish converts, they were familiar with the Scriptures.

An example of the other approach is found in Acts 17:22-34, when Paul met with the educated Greeks on Mars Hill. There in Athens, Paul not only pointed to creation as having an authoritative voice (Psalm 19:1-2), but also quoted well-known Greek poets (sometimes called prophets) who had written things that agreed with the Word of God (Acts 17:27-28). The Spirit of God evidently set His seal on this sermon, because some of the Greeks were converted, including several prominent people (verse 34).

So in dealing with those not familiar with the Word of God, Paul tried first to establish an understanding of the existence and goodness of God—a God who made such remarkable things for them to enjoy (Acts 14:15-17). In Athens, Paul brought his hearers into accountability by announcing that God requires all men everywhere to repent. You might say that he contrasted the overwhelming goodness of God with the sinfulness of man. Paul's next step was to introduce Christ (Acts 17:30-31).

This leads us to consider another principle. We know that Christ was the motivation for Paul's entire being (Philippians 1:21). Yet despite this, he did not mention the Savior during his speech in Lystra. Naturally, if he had been allowed to continue his message, he certainly would have preached about Christ, because salvation is found only in Him (Acts 4:12). In the early stages of his sermon, Paul could not have mentioned the concept of Jesus, because the Greeks had no foundation of understanding about Jesus. The principle is that there is a logical and correct time to introduce new concepts, even the concept that Jesus is the Son of God. The following may help clarify this:

In her autobiography *The Torn Veil,* Gulshan Esther, a Pakistani of the lineage of Muhammed, shares her personal odyssey. Gulshan became lame at an early age, and her father, a devout Muslim, longed to see her healed. He paid large sums of money searching for cures—from doctors in Pakistan to a top specialist in London. But the doctors could do nothing for her.

Finally, Gulshan's father took her to Mecca to kiss the Black Stone, hoping for a miracle—again without result. It was a terrible letdown for both of them. Another tragedy awaited them upon their return to Pakistan. Gulshan's loving father suddenly took ill and died. Gulshan's mother had died when she was a baby, and this loss seemed the climax of all her life's disappointments. In the grip of bitter grief, Gulshan asked God to let her die.

In answer, a low, gentle voice replied, "I am not going to let you die." Gulshan suddenly felt a new freedom to approach God, the Supreme Being.

Unknown to Gulshan, that gentle voice belonged to Christ—someone described in the Muslim holy book, the Koran, as a prophet, or the "son of Mary." Muslims believe they will go to hell if they believe that Jesus is the Son of God. So in this twentieth-century appearance, Jesus chose to reveal Himself to Gulshan little by little.

"I am Jesus, son of Mary," the gentle voice said. "Read about Me in the Koran, in the chapter called the Sura Maryam." In the Koran, Jesus is also depicted as the healing prophet—and Gulshan desperately craved a healing.

If Christ had revealed Himself as anything else on this first appearance, this young descendant of Muhammed probably would have screamed. It was only much later—after Gulshan had read that section of the Koran many times over, and had prayed for Christ to heal her—that Jesus revealed Himself and miraculously healed her. Later, He appeared to Gulshan again, this time with instructions on how to procure a Bible during a period when they were difficult to obtain in Pakistan. After Gulshan's conversion, she became a dynamic Christian with an international ministry. [9]

If we are appalled by not mentioning Jesus from the start, we should remember that God spent 4,000 years preparing the world for the entrance of His Son. And when Jesus did arrive, He would sometimes say, "Shh! Don't tell people who I am just yet!" (Matthew 12:16; 16:13-16,20; Luke 4:41; 9:35-36). There is the right time to talk about Jesus to Muslims, Jews, New Agers, etc. When that time comes, Jesus will be honored more, because those who are skeptical will be more receptive to believe who He really is.

In a sense, Jesus cautioned us about this in His Sermon on the Mount when He said not to give pearls to pigs. The solemnity of this warning became even clearer to me when I recently heard the story of my great-grandfather Tooley during the pioneer days of New Zealand in the 1800s. One day, he went out shooting with a companion, and came upon a wild pig during the hunt. But something went terribly wrong, for in the end, his friend was eaten by that pig! [10]

The Scripture says, "Do not throw your pearls to pigs. If you do, they may trample them under their feet, and then turn and tear you to pieces" (Matthew 7:6). I believe this verse includes a warning (among other things) not to mention Jesus as the Son of God until the proper time with some people. Otherwise, they won't appreciate the pearl of who Jesus really is. They'll just see something being thrown at them and will think it's a stone. Then they'll attack! Unfortunately, I know of a witnessing incident that took place in a foreign country which had a similar disastrous end. People were killed when this principle was not heeded.

You see, truth is more than just facts. Truth is a person—the person of Christ. Jesus gives out information at the time someone can grasp it. Truth needs to be given out in the right manner—in the way that Jesus would share it.

It is not only with Muslims that we should wait for the right time to share that Jesus is the Son of God. This concept is also difficult for many others to accept. One author states that the concept of Jesus being God's Son is totally misunderstood by the Buddhist population. That's because to many Buddhists, "god" is neither omnipotent nor everlasting. In fact, he is seeking enlightenment himself! The term *son of god* would mean someone even more inferior! [11]

Most Buddhists are not "pure" Buddhists, so they believe in spirits of whom they are afraid. One way to introduce Jesus to them is to represent Him as Someone more powerful than any other spirit.

In one sense, it is easier for Hindus to understand that Christ is the Son of God than it is for those from any other religion. Because they believe in so many deities, some Hindus (but certainly not all) are very happy to include Jesus as one of their deities. The problem arises, however, when you say that Jesus is God—to the exclusion of all others. For Hindus to understand that concept, we must wait for the right time in the course of our witnessing.

The problem of introducing Christ to New Agers is closer to home for most of us. Because the New Age movement has its roots in Hindu thought, they generally believe that, "You're a god, I'm a god, and that tree's a god." Accordingly, they can accept Christ as a god, but will say that they are gods, too. It is very hard to get anywhere with New Agers if the groundwork of establishing absolutes is not done thoroughly. We'll cover this in more detail in the next chapter. But no matter who we're talking to, there really is a correct time to introduce the concept that Jesus is God.

A Pattern to Follow

Now that we've covered the basics, let's make a plan for effective witnessing.

First, it's always good to start a conversation with the unsaved in an area of agreement, then move to those areas of potential disagreement. As we start witnessing we should ask ourselves,

Where is this person in relation to the Bible? If he knows about the Scriptures and believes in them, we would be wise to use them. But if he is not familiar with Scriptures, we'll need to use the slower route that the apostle Paul took.

Second, we must discern whether our friend believes firmly in the existence of God. Obviously, most Christian concepts will not mean anything to them if they don't believe there is a Supreme Being. Many people fit into this category. With this kind of person, we need to prove God's existence by using any common ground or any authority we can find.

Third, we should ask ourselves, *If my friend already believes in a Supreme Being, what is his image of Him? Does it need adjusting?* In many cases, it does. Many people believe in God, but their concept of Him is not the same as that described in the New Testament.

To a Muslim, for example, God is not a loving, tender Father, but an omnipotent Being whose emphasis is on judgment. They believe He has predestined their lives. They believe that He will weigh the good and evil deeds of each person on the Day of Judgment with this stipulation: He will forgive those whom He wills to forgive (especially Muslims). The decision to forgive or not will be made on that Great Day depending on His will (which they believe is fickle), not His justice. [12]

We must communicate with Muslims in the area of our common ground. Like them, we believe in the existence of God, we believe in prayer, and we believe in the coming day of reckoning. But from there, it would be wise to help them understand something of God's character, both His love and His holiness. This aspect of evangelism is so important that we will devote a later chapter to it.

Fourth, we should ask ourselves Do they understand the concept of personal accountability? While some people consider God very harsh, others think He forgives and ignores just about anything. Those who think that way have to be told graciously otherwise. Are they now willing to repent?

Fifth, we should consider these questions: Do they know *who* Jesus is? Do they understand why He came? Do they know about

His ministry, teaching, miracles, death, and resurrection? (We cannot take that for granted in today's world.) Does He have the place in their lives that is consistent with the fact that He is God, and that they are to live for Him? (II Corinthians 5:15). In other words, will they give their lives to God by turning from everything they know to be wrong?

The following pages will expand on the truths that we need to share with those who are on different rungs of the "spiritual ladder." We will also talk about different ways of presenting these truths.

7

Proving God's Existence

How do we start witnessing to people who either say they do not believe in the existence of God, or who doubt His existence—people like atheists, "free thinkers," and agnostics? In the book of Acts, it is evident that Paul's favorite strategy was to refer to creation (Acts 14:15-17; 17:22-28; Romans 1:20). Let's look at his approach, then we'll examine several other methods.

The proof of creation

A number of years ago, I spent several months witnessing on the outskirts of Bangkok, Thailand. Many of those with whom I spoke doubted the existence of God, because Buddha was an agnostic. My strategy was to ask, "Who do you think made the world?" They usually replied that they didn't know.

I then began explaining the concept of cause and effect: a banana had to come from a tree, a baby came from a mother and father, and a television set had to be assembled by someone. I sometimes pointed to my watch and asked politely, "What kind of person would you think I am if I told you that this watch made itself?"

I continued, "Suppose I told you that over the process of time, sand in the earth came together on its own and formed the glass of my watch, and metals in the earth emerged and shaped themselves into cogs? Then one day, an ox died. The ox's hide somehow processed itself to become leather, and produced the strap. Later on, the metal buckle just appeared." By then, my friend had gotten my point—no one would accept such an explanation. I had helped him conclude that creation, with all its multiplicity of parts, could not have arranged itself into the world around us.

In this illustration, it's obvious that the watch had to have a human designer. It also confirms that the designer had to be intelligent and skillful. Likewise, the biological and botanical life teeming around us shows that this planet must have been created by someone intelligent: Someone who had a sense of purpose—His purpose and our own.

Let's also consider the complexity of our physical bodies. In his tract *Twenty Minutes to Decide!,* Noel Gibson explains that every part of our bodies is a masterpiece.

> When you read, about one million light sensitive nerve rods and cones in each eye send impulses to the brain by 338,000 nerve cables. When you hear, 24,000 strings vibrate. A grand piano has 240, and is a mechanism 1 million times larger than the human ear. You live, because your heart pumps 40 million times per year, and uses 400 million berri-like structures in the lungs for collecting oxygen and discharging impurities.[13]

There are other wonders about our bodies that we can all marvel at: the workings of the blood, the digestive system, and all the muscles, tissues, ligaments, and nerve endings of our extremely complicated makeup. We can also admire man's ability to reproduce himself. Thinking scientists are awed by our genes. Our physical characteristics and the traits of our personality are contained in something so small that we can't even see it. The magnificence and capacity of the human brain is awesome, and there's much more in the body that defies imagination.

We can also consider the universe around us. It is so vast that it is mind-boggling. Let me try to explain what I mean.

One way of measuring distance across our universe is by using the term *light year.* That is the distance light can travel in a year. Since light travels at 186,282 miles per second, that means it travels almost six trillion miles in a year. At this rate of speed, light travels 7.5 times around earth's equator in one second. It travels the 93 million miles from the sun to earth in just over eight minutes.

The next closest star is Alpha Centauri, which is 4.3 light years away. And it's in the same galaxy! To travel from one side of our galaxy to the other takes light about 100,000 years, and from our galaxy to the next closest one takes two million years. Scientists believe that to go from one side of our universe to the other would take 15 to 20 billion years. How's that for distance?

Having mentioned something of the vastness of the universe around us, we could discuss the number of stars in it. I can still remember being taken to an observatory by my father when I was young. When it was my turn to climb the steps of the huge telescope and peer through the eyepiece, I wasn't prepared for what I saw—a thick mass of brilliant lights against the backdrop of the blackness of outer space.

Our galaxy is called the Milky Way, and scientists think it has about 100 billion stars. And the Milky Way is only one among millions—if not billions—of other galaxies in the universe.

Among these zillions of stars is a tiny planet called Earth, which the Bible says reveals God's skill. It's easy to see why. Remember, our planet is about 93 million miles from the sun. Scientists tell us that if the earth were much farther away from the sun, we would all freeze. But if it were much closer, we would all fry!

Also, the sun we have is just the right kind for us. Types of stars range from dwarf stars, which are relatively small and cool, to blue-white giant stars, which are gigantic and extremely hot. Our sun is average in size, temperature, and brightness. The combination of the type star it is and our distance from it makes it possible for us to live on this planet.

And the synchronization of movement in the universe is incredible. Someone must have planned it! The moon circles Earth every 28 days, but while it is doing that, the earth is revolving around the sun once every 365 days.

That's not all. The eight other planets in our solar system are also orbiting the sun, taking varying lengths of time to do so, and most of these planets have multiple moons circling them. But then consider that our entire solar system moves around the center of the Milky Way, along with the millions of other galaxies! Makes your head feel like spinning, doesn't it?

There are, of course, many other aspects of creation to which we can point, from tasty food to cute kids. Whatever we choose to discuss, we must remember that we are not only trying to convince people of God's existence, but also to inspire them to love Him. A study of creation has the ability to do just that—especially if we speak with a sense of awe and gentleness.

Creation proves God's very existence, and at the same time, colorfully illustrates His loving character (Romans 1:19-20). We will amplify that thought in the next chapter. The existence of the vast universe has at least one other ability as well—it gives men a sense of purpose: there must be some meaning to our lives if Someone went to this much trouble in creating the universe!

The Scriptures declare that creation's "voice has gone out into all the earth, [its] words to the ends of the world" (Psalm 19:4). This is why the apostle Paul considered creation to have an authority. And it does. One day, everyone will be called to account for the response they made to this "voice" which was speaking to them every day.

Talking about creation is one way to prove the existence of God. Let's now look at some other ways.

The proof of conscience

Many people will argue that conscience is merely the result of environment. That assertion is partially true. Our environment does influence our conscience to be dull or sharp. In fact, the Bible suggests that we can each influence our conscience to the degree of even deadening it (I Timothy 4:2). But our environment does not create our conscience.

There was a time in every person's life when his conscience was alive (Romans 7:9). We knew that certain things were wrong, even though people around us were doing them. Before I was a Christian, I had moral convictions—things that flew in the face of the beliefs of those around me. One day, we will each have to answer to God for what we have done with our conscience (Romans 2:14-16).

In his book *Mere Christianity,* C.S. Lewis gives a powerful example of this built-in sense of right and wrong. Lewis says that a quarreling man is appealing to this built-in sense of moral law when he says, "That's not fair!" He's appealing to some kind of standard which he expects others to understand, too. [14]

Another example is seen in the power of the media in exposing public leaders. Have you ever stopped to consider why this exposure has such power? If the people of our nation had no innate sense of right and wrong, exposure of a leader's deeds would have no effect. But because God gave each of us a conscience, exposure carries the potential for public outcry. Even television journalists who say they don't believe in God fit into C.S. Lewis' example when they divulge leaders' secrets over the air. They are appealing to a standard which they expect their listener to share.

So if our consciences appeal to a standard which we expect everyone (despite background or culture) to possess, we are, in effect, confirming the existence of Someone who set that standard in place. If we can get our listeners to agree, it should not be difficult to point them in the direction of the Moral Ruler of the universe.

The proof of logic

I find myself using this element more and more, because so many people have been influenced by the New Age movement, which tends to champion the thought that there are no absolutes.

"Let's suppose there are no absolutes," I might begin. "That would mean that I can steal from you, and everyone around us has the right to steal from whomever they please." I let that sink in before I continue.

"If everybody did just that, the world would be in chaos!" As they concede that point, they are acknowledging (without actually admitting it) that they agree with the fifth commandment, "Thou shalt not steal." I don't quote that phrase, because those obviously Christian words would turn them off. Instead, I say something like, "So there really is a case for having a 'no-stealing' rule."

When people are prejudiced against Christianity, you have to strip yourself of all Christian terminology. That makes it easier for the truth to go home, because they're not building walls against it.

My next question might be, "If we were all to kill each other, where would we be?" After a discussion on this subject, I could conclude: "So there really is need for a 'no-murder' rule, as well." I'll then move on to the question of what would happen if everyone were to lie, cheat, rape, and commit adultery. In this way, they'll agree to most of the Ten Commandments without even knowing it.

Some people today have the attitude that there is no meaning to life, so it doesn't really matter what we do. Through the discussion I just mentioned, we can convince those open to truth that just as there is order in the universe, there should be order in the moral realm as well.

All this points to the conclusion that Someone is in charge, and we must appear before Him and answer to Him one day. One important thing to remember is that many in the New Age movement have been wounded deeply. They are therefore more likely to respond to our compassionate reasoning rather than our harsh arguments.

The proof of personal testimony

Just as a skillful craftsman has many tools at his disposal, so does the Christian who witnesses for his Lord. As we discussed in Chapter Four, he has an authoritative instrument in his personal testimony. The story of a changed life, the evidence of love in an environment of hatred, or righteousness lived out in a sinful society, all point to the existence of a Superior Being. And so do the testimonies of God's miracle-working power in healing our bodies.

God's care and protection of His people also speaks of His reality. Many people can testify that in danger, some unseen force has physically moved them out of the immediate threat, thus saving their lives.

Our son Mark tells of the time many years ago when he made a fort high up in a tree. He slipped, and suddenly, there was nothing much between him and the ground. Yet he was miraculously "pushed" by Someone so that he could grasp a branch and save himself from harm.

My wife and I have seen God's provision many times, and I have noticed that as I've shared these stories—even with the unsaved—it seldom fails to inspire my listeners. While we were based in Davao City, Philippines years ago, we both felt impressed that I should travel to Munich, Germany. YWAM was sponsoring a massive witnessing outreach during the 1972 Olympics. When I waved goodbye to Margaret at the Davao Airport, the only ticket I had was from Davao to Manila. I had no ticket to Europe. And the $15 worth of pesos in my thin wallet were all the money I had.

Once I arrived in Manila, I waited at a friend's house. This wasn't the first time I had trusted for God to provide a ticket, but it was still a test. Since God had told me to go, I was trusting that He would provide. But I had no idea where the money would come from. As I waited, the start of the outreach in Munich drew closer.

Finally, I got a call from Margaret informing me that a letter had arrived from a perfect stranger in Australia—a man whom I have never met to this day. He had no way of knowing of my compelling financial need, yet the check he sent covered the cost of the ticket to Munich, with some money left over. People glibly say there is no God, but when you trust Him for your bread and butter (and plane fares), you know He's there! When you share how God supplies money, it grabs people's attention.

You may not have any dramatic accounts to share. But you'll have your own stories to tell as a result of your own walk with the Lord. As you share sincerely about how God has been involved in every area of your life, people will be convinced that God is real.

A whopping 93 percent of our communication is conveyed through facial expressions, tone of voice, and body language. So let your godly enthusiasm add a new dimension to your words. Also, as you share your testimony with the lost, remember to try to be up to date. The fresher your stories are, the better.

The proof of anthropological research

It is significant that anthropological studies demonstrate that even remote and primitive tribes believe in "something" bigger than themselves. The findings go even further: research points to startling evidence that 90 percent of the cultures throughout the world believe in the *one true God.*

Why is this important? Because it contradicts the beliefs of those who promote the theory of evolution who say man was on earth for millions of years before an aristocracy and then later a monarchy evolved. Only then, they say, could man possibly invent the concept of the "one true God." The finding that 90 percent of the cultures believe in one god so embarrassed evolutionists when they discovered it at the beginning of the 1900s that they kept the research hidden for a while. [15] They just did not want it to be known that the "sky-God" concept was alive and well all over the earth!

There are other convincing arguments against the theory of evolution. First, part of the Second Law of Thermodynamics states that things left to themselves will deteriorate. Order will turn to disorder. Iron will rust, wood will rot, and weeds will grow. (That has certainly been true in my garden while I have been writing this book!) In other words, the world is not getting better and better, as evolutionists would have us believe.

Second, the "missing links" in the evolutionary theory are still missing. No one has ever found fossils to prove the evolutionary process—like the supposed link between anthropoid apes and man.

All men are born with a sense that there is Someone greater than they are. It is a well-known fact that hardened "atheists" have called on God when faced with death. This phenomenon has given rise to the expression: "There are no atheists in foxholes."

So proving the existence of God is our first step in leading men from atheistic backgrounds to salvation. Now we must go one step further and consider God Himself....

8

The Character of God

Although many people believe in the existence of a Creator, not all of them have a good understanding of His personal attributes. Actually, people from pagan backgrounds are not the only ones to fit in this category. There are many from nominal church backgrounds who also need a greater picture of who God is. That's because they think He's a harsh and unyielding tyrant—not someone with a compassionate, father-like, and forgiving character.

In fact, the concept of God being a Father is completely lost on many people. Their dads were strict, distant, or often absent. These fathers either didn't think up ways to have fun with their children, or they didn't let their kids know that they were special. Unfortunately, many people had no father at all. When these people hear it said that, "God is a father," it doesn't communicate an accurate picture.

After all, the image we have of God is colored greatly by the view we have of the earthly authorities over us—particularly the opinion we have of our dads. And our superiors are not the only ones who have contributed to this poor picture of God. Preachers (and those who evangelize personally) who are harsh have also played their part. So for many of us, the concept of a loving God doesn't come easily.

Why all this emphasis on the character of God? Because this is the heart of the Gospel. To know God and love Him, we must first come to Him, and it's the knowledge of who He is that inspires us to do that correctly. I believe that no other reason will completely satisfy God, because no other motivation proves that the unsaved person is coming for unselfish reasons. I'm afraid that too many of us come to God just for what we hope to get out of Him.

The Scripture draws the analogy between a man courting his bride and Christ wooing people to Himself. A potential husband has to prove his unselfish love if he is going to win the heart of a young lady. Otherwise, how could she confidently expect his devotion and protection, despite all difficulties and changing circumstances? When we think of Christ's love for the Church, we see the same thing. There is no question that Christ unselfishly loves people. He is interested in them for their sakes.

But by the same token, unselfish love must also characterize the bride in marriage, or her part in the relationship will not last in the spirit God intended. A young bride does not really love her bridegroom if the only reason she is marrying him is to leave an unhappy parental situation. In tying the knot, she would be loving herself rather than unselfishly giving herself to her partner.

Neither would it be love if the only reason a woman married a man was that he had a knife at her ribs. In the same way, being afraid of going to hell is not real evidence of love for God. But coming to God just to get to heaven is not a pure reason for approaching Him, either.

The only real proof of our love is when we are drawn to God on the basis of His character. As we do this, we come desiring to love and know Him *no matter what.*

I believe this is why God sometimes allows martyrdom when He has the ability to stop such seeming calamities. It helps the rest of us judge whether we really are serving Him for His sake or for our own.

I am convinced this is why the killing of Christians down through Church history has actually increased the numbers of those coming to Christ. As the unsaved watch Christians lay down their lives for Christ, they are convinced that He must be real. Those who come to Christ during these periods of persecution do so to please God—not to gain friends, influence, or material goods. That, of course, is real Christianity. Some of us may even be called upon to lay down our lives one day to help prove to a cynical world that there is a God, and that we really do love Him!

Our job as personal evangelists is to encourage people to know the Lord. The best way I know to do this is to promote His character. If we do, people will be drawn to Him.

With those who have little understanding of Christianity, we obviously must rely on more tangible things to demonstrate our point. As mentioned previously, the subject of creation is one avenue through which God's "invisible qualities—his eternal power and divine nature—have been clearly seen" (Romans 1:20).

Paul says that we can have faith in God's character, because the things He made tell us what He is like. He used common illustrations to prove this point, like talking about food and gladness of heart as we noticed in Acts 14:17. God could have made less appetizing ways of getting the fuel and energy we need for our bodies. But food tastes delicious—even mouth-watering at times—not like foul-tasting medicine, sawdust, or cement!

Think for a moment—how would it be if God had made us with no elbows or knees? Can you imagine how difficult it would be to get into bed each night?

Suppose we were not endowed with the powers of reason, imagination, or memory. We would wake up in the morning having forgotten all that we had ever learned—maybe even where we were or what our name was!

Think of it—what if God had created us without a voice with which to communicate? Suppose we had no abilities to form friendships or use the emotions of joy, love, or anticipation? If we are witnessing to parents, we can point out another act of God's goodness—the awesome ability to have children.

As I have shared these examples in different conversations, I have seen people visibly moved by the revelation of the character of God that these simple things depict. As you share illustrations like these, your listener will start to realize that our God can be trusted, because He is good-natured. You must, however, have a heart full of love as you speak with people in this way. Otherwise, you will be contradicting what you want to convey, which is that God "richly provides us with everything for our enjoyment" (I Timothy 6:17).

Another very real demonstration of God's character comes

through miracles. A few years ago, I attended a city-wide evangelistic meeting in India. With me were some of my students from Kona, Hawaii. After the meeting had finished, the students and I were standing around near the wooden platform.

I heard my name, and turned to see one of the coordinators of the event—a young Indian brother I'd met earlier. With him was a young, sari-clad Indian girl, looking fearful. My friend's slender face was very serious, and his words held a note of urgency as he introduced the girl as Lila. Four days previously, Lila had been accosted by someone who put a Hindu curse on her tongue. Now she'd lost her powers of speech. Could we help?

The students and I began to pray one by one. After we'd being going on like this for about ten minutes with nothing happening, one of the students had an inspiration. Following the student's lead, I asked Lila to remove a fetish from around her neck. By asking her to nod her head in agreement, we led her in the forsaking of the deity which the fetish represented. We began to pray again, and also to praise the Lord. Then it happened—Lila's speaking ability was restored!

Lila was so thrilled that she came back to the meetings many times that week, bringing friends and neighbors with her. The miracle had shown God's character to her, and she wanted to share that with others! (The performing of miracles has always been one of the chief ways the Gospel has spread.)

One day during Jesus' earthly ministry, He approached a town gate just as a coffin was being carried out by a somber group of people. A large crowd accompanied the weeping mother—a widow—who had just lost her only son. The Bible tells us that when Jesus saw the mother, *His heart went out to her,* and He said, "Don't cry." The bearers stood still while Jesus touched the open coffin. Addressing the dead man, He commanded, "Young man, I say to you, get up!" And the young man did just that, and began to talk!

The mother was beside herself with joy. She had seen a display of the beauty of God that was better to her than the glory of a million Hawaiian sunsets. So had the crowd. They were filled with awe, and said, "God has come to help his people." This news about Jesus spread throughout Judea and the surrounding country (Luke 7:11-17). No wonder the Gospel is called the good news (John 3:17).

In the book of Acts, we read of many people—even entire communities—who came to Christ because of the manifestation of God's character revealed through a miracle.

I believe it is important to remember that when we preach the Gospel, we are offering forgiveness of sin—a subject in which people are often very interested. When forgiveness of sin is promised in pagan parts of the world (for example, if a devotee touches some relic, statue, or idol), thousands upon thousands of people show up!

In Western countries, people spend a phenomenal amount of time and money in psychiatrists' offices as they seek freedom from depression, which is often caused by a guilty conscience. People really do want to know how they can be forgiven.

This is where signs and wonders help. When people see God's compassion in a miracle—like the raising of the widow's son—they know God can be trusted for forgiveness!

Of course, there are other ways of teaching the character of God. When we share how He leads us day by day, this demonstrates something of what God is like—personal and loving. In fact, with some people, the only way of getting into a meaningful conversation with them is to share how God guides me.

This is my favorite way of striking up a conversation with a Muslim. Not mentioning Jesus for a while, I ask if they have prayed that day. Normally, they have. Then I meekly and respectfully ask what God told them in prayer. Usually they look stunned, then protest, "But God never speaks to us human beings!"

I then tell them gently that God often speaks to me (usually during my daily devotions). If they allow me, I tell them about the wonderful things that have happened in my life as a result: I have received guidance, my worry has dissipated, people have sometimes been healed, my finances have been provided, and so on. They are amazed! They didn't know how real God could be.

Each time I do this, I usually receive a fresh revelation of just how friendly Muslim people can be. I truly count them as friends.

You may want to attempt this approach with your agnostic neighbors or those steeped in the doctrines of the Jehovah's Witnesses or the Mormons—or even your nominal Christian friends.

I would encourage you to recount stories that reveal what God is like. They are best if they are your personal stories, but they can be just as powerful if they are the stories of those we know personally. Stories from people you don't know can also be useful. Like the story that follows:

Charles Sullivan was driving alone through Los Angeles one dark, rainy night. At the corner of 42nd Place and Hoover Street—where there were no street lights at the time—he brought his car to a complete stop. The location seemed even darker because of the trees bordering both streets. Not seeing any car or pedestrian in sight, Charles released the brake.

As he started to move into the intersection, a man's voice close behind him said very clearly, "Watch it, Charlie!" Instinctively, he stepped on the brake. At that precise moment, a dark sedan without lights, going about eighty miles an hour, zoomed by just in front of his radiator!

Charles knew that he would have been killed if not for that voice. Where had it come from? He switched on the car's inside light. There was no one in the back seat. Getting out of the vehicle, he found no one around. In the distance, he heard the wail of a police car chasing the reckless driver.

Someone had obviously protected Charles. To me, it speaks of the Lord, and I find the following extra information very interesting in the light of our discussion on God's character. Charles was fifty years of age at the time. "No one," he says, "has ever called me Charlie except my father, and he died 35 years ago!"

God could have called out to Charles by using his usual name. But in that split second when God so desperately needed to communicate, He chose that term of endearment from Charles' childhood! This is what God is like, and we need to communicate that somehow as we evangelize. We don't need to use manipulative or fear-invoking tactics.

It is great to tell stories that explain God's heart, but it's even better to conduct ourselves in a way that demonstrates what God is like. On this score, most of us would agree that shouting at the unsaved or using guilt-producing tactics is not the way to woo them to God!

Accordingly, we will be called upon to demonstrate much self-control, and to extend forgiveness to people so they can see this principle at work in us. Let's be looking for ways to put this principle into practice!

Sharing the Scriptures—with those who acknowledge it—is another way of declaring what God is like. In fact, it will be much easier to point out the character of God to those who are familiar with the Bible. Be sure to point people to the stories in the New Testament. After all, one of the reasons Jesus lived among us was so we could better understand what God was like.

In those Bible passages, we also see that Christ demonstrated how we should operate in evangelism. The aspects of the character of God that Jesus portrayed as He evangelized should be those we exhibit. If we look carefully at the many times Jesus was involved in personal evangelism, we will discover just how merciful He was—with sinful Zacchaeus, with the volatile Simon Peter, with the woman at the well, and with the woman caught in adultery.

Let's take a look at Jesus' contact with Zacchaeus. I'm basing the following account on three sources: the scriptural account in Luke 19:1-10, general knowledge of the times, and my own imagination. But in so doing, I have been careful not to contradict any known facts.

One day, Jesus was passing through the hot Jordan Valley on His way to Jerusalem, which lay ahead of Him up in the Judean hills. He had no intention of stopping in Jericho as He passed through. But a large crowd thronged the Jewish Rabbi whose miracles had brought Him national recognition.

The region around Jericho was prosperous at the time, and people were doing well. So, too, were the tax collectors who were gathering money for the Roman government under the leadership of a despised man named Zacchaeus.

Tax collectors were Jews who worked for the Romans, and

were detested as traitors by other Jews. Since they often defrauded their own people (see Luke 3:12-13), they were doubly despised. They were forbidden to serve as witnesses or as judges, and were expelled from the synagogue. [16]

Zacchaeus was well known. He wasn't just a tax collector; he was a chief among them. And, he was very rich.

Despite this, Zacchaeus wanted to take a look at this renowned Rabbi. But as much as he tried, he couldn't see anything through the tightly packed crowd of people who were taller than he. Driven by a compulsion to see this man whom many were calling the Messiah, Zacchaeus ran ahead and shimmied up to a strong branch of a tree beside the dusty main road. There he waited expectantly.

With the crowd around Him, Jesus came closer and closer to the tree, until He was directly underneath. Suddenly, the Lord looked up and called the tax gatherer by name! Then Jesus, His voice so full of acceptance and compassion, asked if He could stay in Zacchaeus' home.

What? Jesus wants to come to my house? thought Zacchaeus, *He doesn't despise me?* He could hardly contain himself for joy!

A new warmth filled his heart, and he resolved right then and there to do something radical. He decided to start a new life, and to give up defrauding people. He'd wanted to do something like this before, but the people had made him feel so guilty and condemned that he could not get near enough to anyone in the synagogue to even talk about spiritual matters. *But this Prophet—He wants to come to my house?*

So Zacchaeus climbed down. Immediately, he heard the crowd murmuring against Jesus for suggesting that He stay in Zacchaeus' house. *All right, then,* he thought, *I'll let them all know about my new resolve!*

"Lord, right now I'm declaring that I'll give half my possessions away. I'm tired of living for money and for myself. It's not worth it. And if I have cheated anyone, I'll pay him back four times the amount I stole!"

When Jesus heard this, tears came to His eyes. This was the kind of repentance He had been preaching about for three years. He was delighted to see yet another person respond to His love before He went to the Cross. And the four-fold restitution? *Well, it's four times what I require,* He thought, *but at least Zacchaeus won't be tempted to cheat again!*

"Zacchaeus," He said, "you're a saved man. You and your household are the very people I came looking for to bless and change."

Many of us today would have thrown Zacchaeus a demeaning line like, "How can you hope to escape the damnation of hell? Look at everything you've done!" But God is not like that. Nor is the Gospel. Otherwise, it would not be good news.

We capture something of the heart of God in Isaiah 57:16, which reads: "I will not accuse forever, nor will I always be angry, for then the spirit of man would grow faint before me...."

Jonah said, "You are a gracious and compassionate God, slow to anger and abounding in love, a God who relents from sending calamity" (Jonah 4:2).

I love this about God! He often looks for that lack in a person, ministers to it, then draws him away from his sin by overwhelming him with His love.

I believe Zacchaeus' need at that time was to be accepted—something that all human beings need, and which Zacchaeus wasn't receiving at the time. This need was met by Christ's unconditional love. That's the love that says, "I love you because of who you are, not because of how you have performed." That's the love of *God.* And it ministers. Instead of sending Zacchaeus away to cringe and hide, it brought out the best in him. It brought him "to his knees" in his heart.

I believe people come to Christ when they have a personal revelation that God is pulling for them—which is what happened with Zacchaeus. By His love, Jesus brought out the Zacchaeus that God had originally created—the noblest-of-all Zacchaeus. In response, the tax collector gave himself wholeheartedly to the Lord. That's Christianity!

It is the character of God—His unconditional love—that motivates repentance. I have the feeling that the reason we have not evangelized the world is not because it cannot be done, or because we haven't spent a lot of energy and money trying to do it. Instead, it's because we haven't shown enough unconditional love. The more of this kind of love we show, the more down-on-the-floor-thumping-the-rug repentance we will see!

Before we finish with Zacchaeus, there are at least two lessons to learn from his story: One is that it's the kindness of God that leads us to repentance (Romans 2:4); the other is that despite God's unqualified love, *we still have to repent.* Not until Zacchaeus proved his repentance did Jesus promise salvation (Luke 19:8-9).

Does that sound confusing to you? Remember, God's love is unconditional. Even on the day of judgment, He will love the lost, and weep as they go to a place of eternal separation from Him. That's just the nature of His cherishing love.

God stands to lose a lot when someone does not make it to heaven. It means that person has not fulfilled the purpose for which they were created. That will hurt God. But salvation is very conditional. You have to repent before you are entitled to that. Heaven wouldn't be enjoyable for anyone who had not repented. Being loved by God doesn't automatically save anyone, but it sure is a powerful motivator.

Is this merciful approach of Jesus restricted just to His dealings with Zacchaeus? No, it isn't. Remember that He used a similar approach with the woman at the well (John 4:1-42).

Time and space do not permit us to have a look at other similar incidents in Jesus' evangelism ministry—like His dealings with Simon Peter (Luke 5:1-11), and the woman caught in adultery (John 8:1-11). Unfortunately, many of us have sometimes witnessed in a way that has forgotten the heart of the Gospel—which Jesus defined as mercy (Matthew 9:12-13; 12:7).

We mentioned earlier that people should not come to Christ simply out of the fear of going to hell. We must, however, be true to the Word of God, and believe in such a place.

Jesus certainly referred to hell in His public discourses. But there is no record through the pages of the New Testament of His mentioning hell in any of His one-on-one evangelism encounters.

As He talked to the woman caught in adultery, to Nicodemus, to Mary Magdalene, to the rich young ruler, or to others, He never used a "You've got to change or else" technique. Through the entire book of Acts, we read of no incident where the apostles used the fear of hell as a "you'll do as I say" device, either.

Then why is hell mentioned in the Bible? The thought of people going to hell is meant to stir us Christians to evangelize. At times, Jesus may have mentioned hell to stir His followers into action rather than to get sinners to repent. This much is for sure: Jesus never used the word hell once when He evangelized one on one.

In the book of Acts, the apostles turned the world upside down without mentioning hell in their sermons even once, and without emphasizing judgment. When dealing with "the man on the street," Jesus and the apostles never resorted to the method of some, who point and pronounce hellfire and brimstone upon the unrepentant. Stern words were reserved for the religious leaders of the day, whom they knew to be hypocrites.

However, this does not mean that we can talk tough to leaders of any religious group. Quite the contrary. Jesus was direct, but not harsh, when He talked to Nicodemus, despite the fact that Nicodemus was a Pharisee. Jesus could see that his heart was seeking truth.

This man was so open that he later defended Jesus before the Jewish internal parliament, which was filled with the Lord's bitterest enemies (John 7:50). Later, he embalmed Jesus' body with an amount fit for a king (John 19:38-40). Jesus' forthrightness with the other Pharisees was because they knew what was right, but didn't live in accordance with it. They were not heathen priests.

If Jesus were on earth today, His stern words would be reserved for any leader of His church who knew the truth, but was not living the truth because of selfishness and pride. He would have strong words to say to leaders who embezzled funds or who had cheated on their wives, yet remained brazenly unrepentant.

But I don't think Jesus would have us speak sternly to priests of non-Christian or pagan religions. In his book *Like a Mighty Wind,* Mel Tari tells the story of how a pagan priest was giving a sacrifice to his "blood god" on the island of Timor—an animist area of

Indonesia. The priest's name was Sam Faet, and he was suffering from leprosy. Sam Faet was before his altar when Jesus suddenly appeared before him.

"I am the God you are seeking," He said. "This is not the way to worship Me."

"Lord, who are You, and how do You want to be worshiped?" the priest asked.

"I will tell you My name and how to worship me later," Jesus said. "First you must gather all your images and witchcraft materials and burn them," Jesus continued. "When you do this, I will visit you again and tell you all about Myself." Then He disappeared.

Because Sam Faet was the high priest, the people obeyed his instructions and burned their gods. This done, Jesus reappeared to the priest and healed him of his leprosy. He now revealed who He was, and gave instructions concerning salvation and the Christian walk.

In turn, Sam Faet shared all this with his people, who willingly accepted his message. When one of the teams from the Timor Revival reached this village, they found an established church, with Christians walking a holy life with Christ. [17]

In the example just given, Jesus dealt gently with the pagan priest, and healed him. This is another application of the principle that the "kindness of God leads you toward repentance" (Romans 2:4). To apply this principle, we have to be very gentle, present God's truth at the appropriate time, and require repentance for salvation.

In review, we can use many ways to describe God's character. The goodness of God as revealed in creation is but one. Seeing or hearing about healings or miracles is another. A third approach is talking about our day-by-day walk with the Lord, and sharing how we hear His voice. In this way, we make God's trustworthy character known. One avenue is the recounting of our Christian experiences or those of other Christians. Another path would be the use of Bible stories, which display just what God is like—especially the account of Jesus' death for our sin.

Jesus showed us that meeting someone's felt need was a very legitimate way, though not the only way, to convince people of His character, and to woo people to Himself. Jesus met the felt needs of the woman at the well, of Zacchaeus, and of Simon Peter (Luke 5:1-11). The Bible gives other examples, as well (Luke 8:2; John 8:3-11; Acts 16:27-34).

But perhaps the greatest approach of all is by personally demonstrating God's character either by exhibiting Christlike tendencies in our own lives, or by praying for and seeing God step into our friends' lives by way of a miracle. Whatever avenue we use, the goal should always be to exhibit the character of God in a way that will motivate people to know Him. After all, that's a description of our job!

9

Man and His Sin

God created man with the ability to love good and to shun evil. We still see this ability expressed today when a complete stranger risks his life defending someone he doesn't know. We see it when a mother gives up desperately needed sleep in the middle of the night to attend to the needs of her baby. We also see it when a son denies himself money, clothing, and even food to compassionately care for his aging parents. But we all know that man has the opposite capability, as well. Our newspapers and television newscasts graphically illustrate this for us every day.

The ability to do either good or evil is couched in a wonderful liberty which we call the power of choice. If man did not have the power of choice, he would be no more than an animal—living, but with no ability to determine his lifestyle or destiny.

By giving us this freedom to choose, God took a risk. It is the same kind of risk we parents take when we decide to start a family. We know that our children have the potential to one day be prostitutes, gangsters, or drunkards, yet it usually doesn't deter us. We trust that our offspring will follow our example and will use their free wills not to live immoral lives. We trust that they will respect the lives and property of others.

It's the same way with God. As much as He longs for our love and allegiance, He is not going to force it out of us. Just as no normal man would get any fulfillment out of forcing a girl to marry him, God would get no satisfaction from "causing" us to love Him. So with a heart bursting with love, God bestowed on us the beautiful creation that we have already described. Then He waited expectantly for our loving response.

Sadly, history records that man has shunned God. Using his

gifts and talents in a destructive way, man has hurt others and himself in the process. The Bible's comment on this is designed to stir our deepest emotions. A friendly, loving God was "grieved that he had made man on the earth, and his heart was filled with pain" (Genesis 6:6, italics mine).

These selfish expressions which hurt God and others are what the Bible calls sin. Let's take a look at just what sin really is.

Everyone knows there is a difference between right and wrong

Earlier, we talked about man appealing to a standard that he expects others to possess, when he protests by saying that something "isn't fair!" This is what C.S. Lewis called oughtness, and it exists in every culture on every continent. But when did this sense of "oughtness" enter the world? Adam and Eve had those instructions written on their hearts, and so has every person who has entered the world.

Several generations before Moses, the wife of an Egyptian official asked a young Israeli named Joseph to go to bed with her. He refused despite the fact that he was lonely and far from home. The woman continued her sweet, seducing remarks day after day, but Joseph steadfastly rebuffed her approaches.

One day, Joseph protested loudly, "How then could I do such a wicked thing and sin against God?" (Genesis 39:9). Sin against God? Remember, the Ten Commandments had not yet been given! But Joseph did not have to wait 400 years for Moses to inform him, "You shall not commit adultery." This law is written on each man's heart. So it shouldn't be hard to point out lovingly that God holds us all to this rule.

When we tell someone not to do something, and then we do it ourselves, we are bringing judgment on ourselves. The Bible warns that every mouth will be silenced, and the whole world will be held accountable to God (Romans 3:19).

Sin is being independent of God

Simply put, the essence of sin is being independent of God. Of course, this independence can be expressed in a myriad of ways. It is finding significance in life without depending on Him. While some people find meaning and comfort through drugs or crime, others worship at the altar of the arts, knowledge, or money, leaving God completely out of their lives. As Christians, we also need to ask ourselves if our lives are being focused on the Lord and the extension and development of His Kingdom.

We will always meet good-living people who will protest that they have done nothing wrong. But the truth is that they have left God out of their lives in many ways, and have not been completely identified with His purpose. These people might even admit that they've looked passively on evil, and have not really tried to make this world a better place.

Sin is a choice

Although we must be compassionate as we witness, we must not allow people to excuse their sin. While it is true that we are in bondage to sin as a result of our disobedience, the Bible teaches that man is accountable for the wrong things he has done which have led him to this sinful slavery.

"Each one is tempted," the apostle James concluded, "when, by his own evil desire, he is dragged away and enticed" (James 1:14). As tough as this may sound, even our deception is our fault. The Scriptures teach that mankind is deceived through disobedience, pride, refusing to love the truth, and taking pleasure in unrighteousness (Obadiah 3; II Thessalonians 2:10-12).

In the midst of our bondage, we feel desperately that "I cannot help myself," or "I was made this way." But it is amazing just how much in control of ourselves we really are.

Do students cheat on an examination when the teacher is watching? Do thieves usually rob a bank in full view of armed security men on duty? Do public leaders commit acts of sexual immorality in the presence of the media? How is it that we can control ourselves on certain occasions, but when we think no one is watching, we suddenly "cannot help ourselves"?

The Bible says that one day, all the books will be opened. On that day, every mouth will be silenced. Mankind will agree with God on how wrong sin really is (Revelation 20:12; Romans 3:19).

If we are speaking to someone who is familiar with the Bible, we can guide them to the words of Jesus in Mark 7:21-23. Jesus lays the blame for our sin on our own hearts—not on our neighbors or on our environment, although we know that these do influence us. But that's just it—they influence us, but don't cause us to sin. Otherwise, it would not be fair for God to punish wrongdoing.

This understanding that each of us is responsible for our own sin was promoted in the 1830s, and was one of the contributing reasons why revivals broke out at that time. In fact, all the revivalists of the 1700s and 1800s, whether Arminian or Calvinist—Charles Wesley, George Whitfield, Charles Finney, and others—stressed man's responsibility (Jeremiah 31:30; Ezekiel 18:4). That's why they saw the results they did. When people are taught responsibility, they are more likely to act responsibly (Ezekiel 18:21-24).

Sin is an attitude, not just an action

Many people may feel that they have not sinned because they have not been involved in murder, adultery, or theft. But the roots leading to those outward manifestations may still lurk beneath the surface. Jesus taught that to hate was to "murder," and to have lust was to "commit adultery" (Matthew 5:21-28). The apostle Paul taught that covetousness was more than theft—it was actually idolatry (Colossians 3:5). In addition, the inward sins of pride, selfish ambition, and jealousy are just as deadly.

Sin does not include only the obvious acts of commission like a caustic remark, an armed holdup, or the intentional taking of human life. Sin is also omitting to do what is right—like not helping to protect another's feelings, or not helping to bear someone's burden of grief. Or it could be not helping those in obvious physical or emotional need, when it is in our power to do so.

Our sin affects others

It is almost impossible to witness for Christ and not be confronted by someone asking, "Why do the innocent suffer?" I believe that it's a grievous error not to take time to answer this concern with genuine feeling. That question sincerely rages in many troubled hearts.

One possible way to respond is to gently say: "If I were to get into a car, disobey the rules of the road, and kill some innocent pedestrian, it would not be the fault of the government that made the rules of the road. It would be my fault. My sin would have caused the innocent to suffer. And if I lie, steal, or get angry, others will be hurt. Innocent people suffer in wars, because man's sin inevitably affects others."

A recent UNICEF television documentary declared that a child dies every two seconds somewhere in the world. The program also said that with current scientific knowledge, we could defeat the five top causes of child malnutrition in almost every developing country. The total cost would be an extra $2.5 billion a year. But that's not much when you consider that much is spent on the military every single day around the world. [18]

Before the United Nations troops went into Somalia, a television news program showed footage of tons of rice and flour sitting idle in warehouses beside the docks in Somalia. At the same time, people were dying of starvation in the surrounding countryside. At that time, two million Somalis were in danger of dying. Yet the international community had supplied enough food to feed all these people for several weeks.

The news commentator explained that roving bandits threatened even the aid workers, and they hijacked trucks carrying food to the people. The United Nations said that they did not have the armored cars for their protection. In the meantime, Somalis were dying at the rate of nearly 2,000 a day. [19] That situation led to United Nations troops eventually going into Somalia to help restore order.

After sharing some of these observations with the person to whom you are witnessing, you can gently conclude that it's obvious that man's sin is responsible for the suffering and anguish in our world.

Your listener may agree, but many will go further and ask, "Why couldn't God come up with a different system so that innocent people don't get hurt by my wrong choices?" The way I deal with that question is to take them to the thought expressed at the beginning of this chapter.

As parents, we expect that our children will honor our example of fair play and decency. I might point out further that parents could easily overcome their children's free wills by injecting the children with a substance that would make them vegetables. In that way, the parents could ensure that their children would never do anything wrong. But who would ever think of doing something like that? Free will, with all its risks, is better that no free will at all. No one wants to be a robot, or to create a robot.

The way we conduct ourselves during a discussion like this is important. If our friend sees that we are genuinely interested in his grievances, we'll better display what God's character is really like.

We Christians must proclaim two glorious aspects of God's nature: that He is innocent (He has done nothing wrong), and that He cares very deeply about people's hurts. I often try to insert something about the tender miracles of our God into a conversation on this subject. I might talk about the sufferings of someone I know, and tell my friend how God either healed that person or gave him the help he needed to get through his awful ordeal.

If I feel it's appropriate, I might point out that in times of war and famine, Christians who are motivated by God's tender love are usually the ones who deny themselves emotionally, physically, and financially, and rush to meet the needs of those have been affected. The aim of all this is that I want my listeners to understand that God gets involved in taking away suffering and pain when He can justly do so. Jesus' life on earth was a glorious example of this (Acts 10:38). And no one has suffered more wrongly than Jesus did when He died on the cross.

Now that we understand what sin is, I want to stress the attitude we should have when we talk about sin. Although mankind is to blame for the suffering in our world, God never gives us the cold shoulder and walks away. He weeps with us, knowing our hurt. He wants to take away the load we are carrying, and to remove the burden of our guilt. What a God!

We must strive diligently to represent this aspect of God's

character as we talk about sin. Remember, this is an area where people are usually very sensitive. Speak so that those listening to you will feel they could trust you with the worst possible information about their sinfulness—and still feel that you care for them.

We must not "rub it in" by our attitude of harshness or self-righteousness (Galatians 6:1). People are basically proud, and do not easily acknowledge their sin. We only make it harder for them to admit their wrongdoing if we use condemning language, or if we come across with the attitude, "I could never have done that!"

You may have heard it said that, "We must present the bad news before we present the good news of the Gospel." This means that people won't appreciate the opportunity of forgiveness until they feel guilty over their sins. For years, I accepted that as the undisputed truth, but I don't anymore.

A study of Jesus' one-on-one witnessing experiences reveals that although He was upfront about sin at times, in other instances He used an entirely different approach (as we noted in the last chapter). Sometimes He didn't say one word about sin, yet He saw people repent deeply. So what should be our rule of thumb?

We all know that to be saved, we must acknowledge our sin. Some people will readily admit their wrongdoing, but it's much harder for others.

Jesus demonstrated that Christians can help people be more willing to acknowledge their sins. An accepting, loving Christian (the kind whose eyes mist up as he listens to someone's problem) is the one who will help the reluctant person immensely. People often will open up much more if they know they will still be loved and accepted.

This is how Zacchaeus felt in front of Jesus. That's why he repented. But unless others sense that we love them, I don't think we can expect them to break down under the conviction of sin in our presence.

The poorer the self-image the sinner has, the softer the soul winner's heart must be. The reason is quite simple. A certain level of self-esteem is necessary in order to bare one's heart before the Lord. One of the ways to build up a person's self-esteem is for him to feel our unconditional acceptance. This explains why Jesus spoke compassionately to the woman at the well, to Zacchaeus, and to Simon Peter (Luke 5:1-11).

Of course, Jesus was more direct with Nicodemus (John 3), and even more so with the rich young ruler, although Christ remained very loving (Mark 10:21). That young man obviously loved things more than he loved God's will for his life. Maybe Jesus was more direct with those two because their self-esteem was more intact.

But don't misunderstand me. No one can say at the Judgment Day, "I'm going to hell because no one loved and accepted me." They can't say that, because the whole of creation proclaims that there's a loving God in the universe. Later, we'll see that the Cross of Christ says the same thing. Even so, when a struggle rages in a sinner's heart on whether to follow God or go his own way, tender-hearted counseling can tip the scales in the right direction.

But we must clearly understand one fundamental truth. According to Scripture, *sin must be repented of for salvation to occur.*

During those conversations in which I sense that it is right to talk about sin, as opposed to waiting, I have found that if I mention some of my former sins, it helps my friend to acknowledge his transgressions. However, I have to exhibit the solemnity that befits the fact that I've grieved God and wounded others. At the same time, I must demonstrate a soft spirit that will tell my friend that he can share his heart—that he lied, stole, was violent, or was immoral.

As a general rule, guys should not share about their former sexual misdeeds to a girl in a witnessing situation and vice versa. In fact, in most non-Western countries, you shouldn't be witnessing one-on-one to a member of the opposite sex at all.

It is also good to gently mention some sins you've never struggled with. This is so the Holy Spirit can softly touch your friend's heart. After all, Jesus said that the Holy Spirit would convict the world of sin (John 16:8). We were all born with consciences. But through constant misuse, your friend's conscience may not be functioning very well. The Holy Spirit can take the words you speak in love, and start the process by which he becomes aware that certain things are indeed wrong.

You might want to ask in a kind way, "Do you get angry sometimes?" That is often a useful question, because most of us have lost our tempers at some time or other. Explain that there is a small inner voice that tells us not to do things, yet we have deliberately gone ahead and done them anyway.

I am sure you will agree that we are not called to the ministry of condemnation. And we should never rejoice when we hear another Christian say something like, "I really gave it to them!"

When we travel from a Western nation to a non-Western nation (or if we work in a non-Caucasian suburb in a Western city), our need for a soft heart is intensified. Whether we like it or not, white-skinned people often represent the colonial powers that formerly ruled their country—a Western nation that may have governed unjustly.

It is common knowledge that more than a hundred years ago, Great Britain forced China to open its doors to trade when it defended British merchants who were illegally importing 20,000 chests of opium. This led to a war which Britain had no difficulty in winning. We know there are always two ways to look at things, but Mexicans can feel hurt even today by the way they were forced to cede California and those nearby States to the U.S.

In Asia, Africa, the Pacific, and South America, many injustices were perpetrated by the colonial powers. The hurts of those wounds have sometimes been passed on from generation to generation. If we preach condemnation upon non-Westerners with vigor and insensitivity, it will diminish our ability to be a tool in the hands of the Holy Spirit.

Remember that the West does not have a great track record to boast about in other areas of life. Western countries have a high incidence of AIDS, an unbelievably high divorce rate (even among Christians), and are responsible for moral pollution exported via motion pictures, magazines, and tourist trade. Western nations like the U.S., Europe, Canada, Japan, Australia, New Zealand, and South Africa, all have levels of moral decadence. So we are obligated to talk about sin with a very soft heart—the kind of heart that God intends us to have.

10

A Question to be Asked

During the last few chapters, we discussed the existence of God, the character of God, and man's built-in knowledge of right and wrong. Since God's Word states that these three things are clearly evident to every person, we will be held accountable for what we do with this knowledge. Whether a person was raised in church or is a drug addict, murderer, gambler, drunkard, adulterer, or a member of a remote jungle tribe, he is answerable to God for having been aware of at least these three truths.

How can God have a righteous way of dealing with those who have never heard of Jesus? According to His Word, it's not the amount of knowledge you have, but your response to the knowledge you have. If a man from a remote tribe starts living up to the knowledge he has, and wants to know more about the Lord, God will reward him by giving him further revelation.

Stories are told of pagans who cried out to God, received revelation, and came to understand about Christ. That happened because salvation is only found in Jesus (Acts 4:12). Their seeking God has often led to their eventual conversion, just as Sam Faet in Timor came to know the Lord.

However, this should not be used as an excuse for not going to the heathen. How many of us would have come to faith by being desperate enough in our seeking of God to be granted a vision? A God who loves the whole world tells us that we are to go and spread His message everywhere. And because we are filled with His love, we want to bear testimony to Him.

We come now to an important juncture in our witnessing. We have been following a planned approach—a systematic presentation of gospel truth in a logical sequence. In this approach, we might now encourage our friends in a kind way to think about their accountability.

Have they been living consistently with the overwhelming evidence about God's great love for them? Politely ask: "How can someone get to know a righteous and good God when he's sinned so deliberately against this God?" At this point, pause in the conversation. Let the Spirit of God speak to him, and let him think.

While he is thinking about what you've said, he could easily be coming to the realization that he must do something. Remember, without conviction there can be no repentance, and without repentance there can be no salvation (II Corinthians 7:9-10). On many occasions, when a conversation has lapsed into small talk, I have found that asking the above question has brought a listener back face to face with the problem of his sinful soul and his need to find a solution.

As an answer to that question, some people will say that if they "just pray," God will forgive them. If they say that, perhaps we could pose another question: "Suppose a man murdered someone, was tried in a court of law, was found guilty, and was sentenced to be executed. Would it do any good for him to fall down before a human judge and pray, 'Please forgive me!'?"

This is a question I have often asked my listeners, and their usual answer is, "The judge cannot just forgive him and let him go." They obviously feel that public justice would not be served if a criminal goes scotfree. That would only encourage people to commit crimes, and the government would find it quite difficult to maintain law and order. At the same time, the rise in criminal activity would make the people feel very insecure. We need to tell people that God cannot forgive us merely on the basis of prayer.

Something has to happen to us internally before God can justly forgive those of us who have been deliberate sinners. Allow this truth to sink in. Many people fail to see that God would have been just to condemn the world and punish all of us for our sin. Technically, God was not obligated to provide a way for us to be forgiven. However, because of who He is, He provided a solution that allows us to see a full expression of His character—both His love and His righteousness. We will see this unfold as we move on.

Having mentioned the *planned approach,* I have found that in witnessing there is also what I would call the *inspirational approach.* While presenting the scriptural concepts in the sequence I've mentioned, I am always prepared to interrupt the pattern should I suddenly feel a burst of inspiration or revelation to do so. I will explain this more fully later, but in the meantime, we will continue to outline the planned approach, and to consider the next subject of just who Jesus is.

11

Jesus Christ and the Atonement

It is now time in your conversation to introduce the all-important person of Jesus Christ. The Bible tells us that Christ existed before anything was created, that everything came into existence through Him, and that everything holds together by Him (Colossians 1:16-17). Jesus is the exact representation of the being of God (Hebrews 1:3), and is the only One through whom anyone can be saved (Acts 4:12).

However, these concepts are diametrically opposed to the beliefs of many skeptics, radicals, and those from areas of the world which have not been traditionally Christian. Sharing the truth of the deity of Christ too soon is like awakening someone on a pitch-black night by shining a flashlight directly into their eyes. After all, as we said earlier, God spent 4,000 years preparing the world for the advent of His Son. So how should we go about presenting this all-important truth that Christ is the essence of who God is?

One approach is to take our listeners gradually through the steps of the last few chapters—not mentioning the name of Christ to begin with. When I have done this, there is usually such an appetite for the truth that when I have introduced the person of Christ, there has been no resistance. When they follow my argument logically, they sense that Christ must be who the Bible says He is.

By using this approach, I have seen Muslims be totally open to what I say. (An important key for reaching people like these is to avoid trying to prove Christ's deity to them in front of their friends and relatives. Without pressure from others, they will be much more open to truth.)

Another route is to start a friendship with the person. He will learn to respect you, and will listen to you and trust your judgment—particularly if he is open to truth and sees something real about your walk with God.

I am reminded of a story on the "700 Club" television show that has stuck with me. The interview told of a zealous Christian lady in California who witnessed to a young Muslim immigrant from the Middle East. This man thought she was a bit weird. Judging from what the man said, this dear lady broke a lot of the rules for witnessing to Muslims, and he mocked her behind her back.

But two things kept him listening. One was that she kept on buying hamburgers from his street bar, and he didn't want to lose her business. The other was that she asked him if he had things she could pray about. To be polite, the young man kept giving her prayer requests—and he kept seeing answers to those prayers! He grew to respect her life, and started believing her message. Finally, he did the unthinkable for many Muslims—he gave his life over to the lordship of Christ! The young man had seen something real about the lady's walk with God.

Another useful way to present Christ to those who are antagonistic toward the Gospel is through the performing of miracles (or what is commonly known today as the exercise of *power evangelism.*) In the Scriptures, we read of how the Jewish elders were opposed to the doctrines of the early apostles. The healing of the man at the temple gate resulted in 2,000 more people believing that Jesus was God, despite the repeated threats by the Jewish leaders (Acts 3:1-4:4). The miracle had either changed the people's minds or had overcome their previous fear of following Christ.

Yet another way to introduce Christ is to do it slowly—more or less the way God did. First, you could tell the story of His coming as a defenseless baby in a manger. Next, move on to the time when Jesus was twelve years old and asked questions of the elders in the temple, then speak of His preaching. You could go through a number of Jesus' activities: His teachings, His compassion, and especially the miracles He performed—they revealed His glory and deity. You could then share the miracle of His Resurrection, which proves Him to be the Son of God (Romans 1:4).

There is one more way you could go about introducing Christ. A person with an open and logical mind might profit from a discussion on one of the claims of Christ like, "I and the Father are one" (John 10:30). That's a big proclamation. You could ask your friend, "Was He a myth—someone who really didn't exist at all? Was He deceived? Was He lying, or was He telling the truth?" Let's look at all these possibilities.

Was Jesus a Myth?

Over the last few years, radical Hindus have claimed that a present-day Muslim mosque in the North Indian town of Ayodhya stands on the site of a former Hindu temple dedicated to the one Hindus call "Lord Ram." The Muslims have fiercely defended their mosque, and many lives have been lost in the ensuing riots. Wishing to be reasonable, the Muslims have said: "Prove to us that Ram existed, and we will dismantle our mosque." The radicals replied, "We cannot prove that—we just believe!"

Does the life of Jesus fall into that category? Hardly. There are many historical references to Christ by those who lived during or just after Jesus' earthly existence. He was counted in a Roman census. Both secular and religious historians mentioned Him. Writers like Tacitus, Suetonius, Pliny the younger, and a very famous Jewish historian called Josephus refer to Jesus. [20] All the New Testament writers do, as well. That disqualifies Him from being a myth.

Was Jesus Deceived?

In the 1880s, Mirza Ghulam Ahmad of little-known Qadian town (then in British India), claimed to be Christ returned to earth—even though the Scriptures plainly teach that when Jesus returns, the whole earth will see Him (Revelation 1:7). Since Ghulam was deceived on that point, would you believe his other teachings? That's an important question.

Many people are prepared to accept Jesus as a great teacher, but say that they cannot accept His claims to deity. But how can they put confidence in the teachings of a person who says that He is the Almighty when they don't believe it? They can't. If He were deceived about something like that, think about all the other things He could be wrong about.

But consider the characteristics that Jesus had which are not usually associated with deceived people: the high level of Jesus' morality, His clear thinking, and the things He said which "witness with our spirits." Like, "Do to others what you would have them do to you" (Matthew 7:12).

No wonder those who were sent to arrest Him came back empty-handed, saying, "No one ever spoke the way this man does" (John 7:46). One of the additional ways I know that Christ is God is that what He taught confirms everything that nature preaches, and that my conscience upholds as true. That is, it confirms that God's character is kind and just.

Then think of how Jesus did not have the other characteristics of someone who is deceived—like being excessively defensive or withdrawing from reality. Think also about the way Jesus was concerned for His mother when He was on the cross. He asked the apostle John to take care of her after His death (John 19:25-27). A deeply deceived person would not be that unselfish and caring.

Was Jesus a Liar?

Jesus' unique claim to being God was not tied to His miraculous powers alone. Human beings have wrought similar miracles. But central to His claim to deity is His declaration that He would rise the third day after He was crucified. If He didn't rise from the dead, He would have been a liar.

A British journalist saw this very point many years ago, and set out to do research to prove that Jesus Christ did not rise from the dead. The result of his study was the book *Who Moved the Stone,* in which he traced his search to disprove the Resurrection. But his research confronted him with the evidence: Jesus did indeed rise from the dead. [21]

One powerful confirmation for the Resurrection is the empty tomb and the missing body. Some have said that the disciples must have stolen it. That would be hard to believe because they didn't have much chance to do that—soldiers guarded the tomb.

But suppose that the disciples, in their zeal (which they certainly didn't have at the time of Christ's crucifixion), found weapons, overcame the soldiers, and took Jesus' body. Would they have gone through all the persecution they endured for what they knew to be a hoax? Would Stephen and James have died for preaching the Resurrection when they knew where the body of Jesus was? That doesn't make sense.

"Then the Jews must have stolen it," some people have said. But that's hardly logical either, because the Jews would have brought out the body of Jesus for all to see. It would have put the apostles to shame, and would have closed the case once and for all. Nobody would have believed the apostles or would have become followers after that. And the Romans? They would have loved to have had the body, because it would have rid them of the "sect of the Nazarene," which they believed was stirring up trouble by being a threat to Caesar worship.

Was Jesus Telling the Truth?

The greatest proof that Jesus is indeed God is His triumphant resurrection from the dead, which is recorded in the Bible, and is attested to by historical documentation. Josephus, the ancient historian, wrote this concerning Christ in about 93 A.D:

> Now there was about this time, Jesus, a wise man, if it be lawful to call him a man, for he was a doer of wonderful works,—a teacher of such men as receive the truth with pleasure. He drew over to him both many of the Jews and many of the gentiles. He was [the] Christ, and when Pilate, at the suggestion of the principal men among us, had condemned him to the cross those that loved him at first did not forsake him, for he appeared to them *alive* again the third day as the divine prophets had foretold these and ten thousand other things concerning him; and the tribe of Christians, so named from him, are not extinct at this day[22] (italics mine).

What about those who claim to accept the Bible, yet have difficulty believing that Christ is God? What Scriptures should we show them? In addition to that verse in John 10:30 which I already mentioned, here are some other passages:

In Romans 1:4, we read, "[He] was declared with power to be the Son of God by his resurrection from the dead: Jesus Christ our Lord." The apostle John opened his gospel with the statement, "the Word was God" (John 1:1). Further in that chapter, we read that the apostle was referring to Jesus Christ when he mentions "the Word" (1:14). The same apostle refers to the term *Word* in the book of Revelation, which he also wrote. There the term is equated with the King of kings and Lord of lords (Revelation 19:13,16).

The writer of Hebrews tells us that the angels of God are to worship Christ, yet we are told throughout the Bible that no other than God is to be worshiped (Deuteronomy 6:13; Matthew 4:10; Revelation 19:10). The Scriptures also reveal that Jesus Christ is the image of God, and is identical to Him (Hebrews 1:3; Colossians 1:15; 2:9). Hebrews 1:8 says: "But about the Son he says, 'Your throne, O God, will last for ever and ever.'" Then in Acts 20:28, Paul calls the blood of Christ the blood of God, thus equating Jesus Christ with the Almighty.

The Holy Spirit convinces men about the truth of Christ's word. He will endorse what we say about His deity if the listener has an open heart, and if we present the truth while exhibiting the character of God (John 16:13-14; 16:8-11; Galatians 6:1).

The Holy Spirit will also endorse the testimonies of Christians who have been transformed from lives of vice and immorality as a result of following Jesus as Lord. But the Bible does say that some people have a veil over their eyes. In these cases, spiritual warfare has to be waged, for we do not wrestle against flesh and blood, but against principalities and powers (Ephesians 6:12).

The analogy of wrestling is appropriate, because spiritual warfare can be like a wrestling match. As Joy Dawson puts it, the victory is not often won on the first round, or necessarily during the second or third. [23]

Although Jesus was God, and came from heaven, this does not automatically put the world right with God. It wasn't that God found it difficult in His heart to forgive us. But His problem is the need to uphold justice and preserve law and order while extending forgiveness. Many people may not appreciate His dilemma, but the following story may serve to make this more clear.

There was once a king called Zeleukas who made a law that if anyone was found guilty of committing adultery, both of their eyes would be plucked out. Later, a young man broke that law and was brought before Zeleukas. Imagine the pain in the king's heart when he saw that it was his own son! Zeleukas naturally wanted to forgive him, but immediately saw his dilemma. If he acquitted his son, the people would think the law meant nothing, and it would become harder to enforce the law. On the other hand, how could he possibly take out the eyes of his own son?

After painful deliberation, the king came to a decision. He could not waive the law to accommodate his son, as much as he desperately wanted to. So the day for the punishment arrived. Both the king and his guilty son presented themselves before military officers appointed for the task. With a crude knife in hand, a tall, battle-scarred soldier approached the son. The chilling silence was soon shattered by a piercing scream as one of the young man's eyes was gouged out. The tall, well-built soldiers had to hold him still.

The king then motioned for the man in charge to continue. But the soldiers were aghast when their king indicated that they were to remove one of his own eyes! Those watching from the gallery gasped in shock.

After a quick, whispered conference with the king, the officer in charge lifted the bloodstained knife. The soldiers moved to hold the king, and with a swift movement, the king's eye was removed. Grimacing in agony and covering his now-empty eye socket with a shaky hand, King Zeleukas walked slowly back into the palace.

Those in the gallery turned to look at each other, shaking their heads in shocked disbelief. Then slowly, the gallery came alive with conversation. It was the talk of the town for many days. Soon, the logic of the king's move became very clear. He had extended partial forgiveness, but at great cost to himself. At the same time, he laid a foundation to last for a lifetime. That foundation was the people's respect for both the lawgiver and the law.

In this story, we can only imagine the impact that the king's suffering had upon his son. It would not be hard for us to believe that the son was extremely humbled over his father's sacrifice. In love for his father, and in gratitude for still having his sight, I can imagine the young man resolving to never be immoral again. But consider also the moral force that would have extended throughout the kingdom. Wherever the king traveled—now partially blind—it was a clear reminder that he had unswerving moral standards.

The problem King Zeleukas faced was very similar to the one God had to solve. Although He loved man and was committed to doing the best possible for him, He still had to uphold His righteousness, which is also built on love. God knew that sin could never be encouraged, because it hurts others and ultimately brings forth spiritual death. Sin also denies His own character. So what could He do?

His answer was the shedding of blood. To help humble man's proud, sinful attitudes right from the Garden of Eden, God instituted this method. Imagine the trauma our first parents must have endured soon after they sinned. They had to witness the deaths of some of the very animals they had loved and named. The killing of these animals was necessary to provide the garments made of skin that God gave them in exchange for their fig leaves (Genesis 3:21). Think how Adam and Eve must have wept over the loss of these precious, innocent animals. They may have resolved never to disobey God again.

Many people fail to see God's tender overtures to woo Adam and Eve back to Himself in this garden story. God's first desire is not punishment for punishment's sake. He is never vindictive. God's first reaction to sin is to love the sinner into repentance. God always plans to redeem a man to his original purpose.

The Lord continued to humble men lovingly over the centuries through the shedding of animal blood. "Without the shedding of blood, there is no forgiveness" (Hebrews 9:22). God instituted this practice to inspire mankind into loving submission by encouraging an internal work to be done deep in the heart of man. God never wanted merely to provide a right legal standing. The annual Day of Atonement is a fitting example of what I mean.

Think with me about the effect that the Day of Atonement had upon the lives of children in a typical Jewish home. Three weeks before that great day every year, the father brought home a little lamb for the coming sacrifice. The children fell in love with the animal, and played with it at every opportunity.

When the day of the sacrifice came, they wept as they learned that the lamb was going to be offered. They were heartbroken at the mere thought of the slaying of their precious, woolly friend. But as the children watched the crimson blood spurt out as the little, white lamb struggled for its life, we can all understand how they must have felt.

A good father would have used the occasion to reinforce the concept of how awful sin is to God. Deep impressions were made upon those little hearts on each Day of Atonement. These memories would not be erased easily. The children must have thought, *My sin must be horrible for it to cause the death of my pet.*

We know from Scripture that the blood of these animals was not the only condition to be met for the person to be cleansed of his sin. It was also necessary that the worshiper respond to the shedding of the blood with repentance.

The prophet Micah asked the people of Israel if the Lord would be pleased if they sacrificed thousands of rams. By implication, Micah said that really wouldn't be enough. What would please God would be the things produced in the heart of the offerer through the shedding of the blood, as well as the offering itself. That, Micah concluded, involved the offerer acting in righteousness, having a forgiving attitude toward others, and walking in humility before God (Micah 6:6-8). If the sacrifice produced the necessary brokenness of heart, and persuaded the offerer not to sin again, God's purposes were fulfilled.

The psalmist conveyed the same thought when he declared, "You do not delight in sacrifice, or...in burnt offerings. The sacrifices of God are a broken spirit; a broken and contrite heart, O God, you will not despise" (Psalm 51:16-17). Through the shedding of blood, God was *just* by discouraging sin, and *merciful* by forgiving freely.

It is important to note that for centuries, the normal Jewish mode of execution was by stoning. Several carefully aimed rocks could easily have killed Jesus Christ. But God chose the awful cross. Why? God wanted to inspire brokenness of heart in the people, in an even greater way than through offering animal sacrifices. He deliberately made it horrible so it would humble the heart of man over sin, and deter him from sinning again. He also wanted us to overflow in gratitude for Christ's suffering, and to treasure fellowship with God because of the cruel death He endured for us.

The fact that God sent Jesus Christ to save man from his sin is an awesome revelation of different aspects of His character. It upholds the principle of justice because sin is discouraged. We can now understand why God instituted the practice of shedding blood to illustrate that sin is horrible. Alas, many modern people have lost this concept. We won't have revival until this principle is recaptured, not by legalistic ways like offering animal sacrifices, but by being overwhelmed by the love and holiness of God.

The Cross also demonstrates God's determination to find a way to be merciful. The Bible says that the blood of Jesus Christ, God's Son, cleanses us from all unrighteousness as we walk in the light (I John 1:7). That, my friend, is the God we must present to the public. It is another reminder why we must always present Christ with love and compassion. When we don't, we spoil the purpose of the Cross.

We must also understand that the biblical sacrifices are quite different from the sacrifices performed by pagans. In heathen sacrifices, sin is dealt with in a way which allows the offerer to continue in his sin. Since a sacrifice has been offered, the sinner believes that he's starting fresh, but has made no commitment to stop his sin. Jesus' death provides a way out of our sin, but we are not free to continue in willful sin just because Jesus died. Humbled and broken by His substitutionary death, we rise from our knees, completely changed to live in righteousness and communion with God.

If you have been following the suggested witnessing pattern of this book, you have shown your friend much of the pathway back to God. At this stage, many Christians would ask for a committal to Christ by using the old phrase, "Do you want to accept Jesus?" But I would not suggest this. It is so easy for the listener just to say "yes" to please you, especially in some parts of the world. Many people believe that the term *truth* does not mean "the real facts," but rather what they think their listeners want to hear. (See Chapter 17 for a further discussion on this subject.) So instead, try asking questions in such a way that a "yes" or "no" answer is impossible. Ask questions that require a thoughtful answer of at least one sentence. A good way to do this is to use phrases that commence with the words *what, where, why, who*, and *how*.

Instead of asking if they want to "receive Jesus," you might say kindly, "You have heard what we have said about God, about sinful men, and about the Lord Jesus Christ. What do you think your response should be to all this?" If the listener does not offer an answer, perhaps he or she is not ready for salvation.

If the listener does indicate that he wants Christ and forgiveness, it is wise to mention the topic of repentance. So far, we have talked about God's initiative in salvation. Now we must deal with what God requires of us all.

12

Repentance

As we have seen, Jesus made provision for the forgiveness of our sin. But this does not automatically make you and me right with God. Our response to Christ's sacrificial death on the cross is all important, as the following story will make clear.

George MacIntosh (not his real name) had been condemned to death by a U.S. court for committing a violent crime. Awaiting the day of execution, he sat in his cell on death row. George had a caring friend on the outside. This man had considerable influence with the State Governor, and obtained a pardon for George.

George's friend excitedly took that pardon to the prison, anticipating the delight on George's face. But instead, George refused to accept the pardon! No amount of pleading would change his mind. Finally, his friend walked slowly away from the prison, his drooping shoulders reflecting his disappointment.

This left the authorities in a dilemma. What happens if a man's release is granted but he refuses to walk out of jail? A special court session was called, and after careful deliberation, the decision was handed down: "The pardon is valid only if the condemned man receives it." After the execution, no one was sadder than the friend who had worked for George's release.

The parallel of that story is striking. Although Jesus worked for our salvation, forgiveness cannot take effect until we submit to His loving lordship. These are His terms, and they are truly just. When people refuse God's loving overtures and miss out on His pardon, no one is sadder than God. He will bear the loss of their fellowship for all eternity.

We shall endeavor to go very carefully into this subject of what God requires of man. I believe that it is at this point that many of our mistakes are made in witnessing. We have a tendency to rush in and pray the sinner's prayer with someone before they are ready.

If you have been witnessing to someone following the pattern suggested in this book so far, you will be coming close to leading that person to Christ. At this point, it would be an advantage if your friend has accepted the authenticity of the Bible, as we are going to rely heavily on its authority. Although the following is explained in detail, only the gist of what is said here will need to be shared with an inquirer.

Our first consideration has to do with the word *repentance*, which means forsaking things we know are wrong. Repentance is different from confession, which is admitting that we have sinned. Repentance is forsaking that sin.

Turn from Sin

We have already looked at the subject of sin in some detail, and see that it is actually selfishness. It is also rebellion. Let's look at the fruits of this rebellious heart against God.

The apostle Paul was led by the Spirit three times to list sins which, if not repented of, will exclude us from God's Kingdom (Galatians 5:19-21; Ephesians 5:5; I Corinthians 6:9-10). The apostle John records a supplementary list in Revelation 21:8.

Familiarizing ourselves with these passages of Scripture would be an asset to our understanding of what God considers wrongdoing. Note that sexual sins and the worshiping of idols are mentioned in each list, while stealing, lying, witchcraft, murder, hatred, jealousy, slandering, and wild parties also are mentioned. To repent is to make a deliberate, conscious act to leave these things behind.

Turn from the World

The apostle John wrote, "Do not love the world or anything in the world. If anyone loves the world, the love of the Father is not in him" (I John 2:15). James 4:4 says, "Don't you know that friendship with the world is hatred toward God? Anyone who chooses to be a friend of the world becomes an enemy of God." (See James 1:27; Romans 12:2.)

But what do these Bible writers mean by the term *world*? It cannot indicate separation from the people of the world, because Matthew threw a dinner party after his call to be a disciple—a gathering to which many despised tax collectors and other sinners were invited, and Jesus mingled freely among them (Matthew 9:10-11). The world from which we are to be separated is the system of rebellion and living without God. The apostle John describes this evil system in three ways, and tells us to keep ourselves from it (I John 2:16, NASB). Here are the three phrases he uses:

The Lust of the Flesh

In this context, *lust* means excessive participation in deeds of the body. We all know that eating and drinking are God-given pleasures in which we are to participate. But we also know that gluttony and drunkenness are sins.

Sexual relationships are another God-given joy (Proverbs 5:18-23), but sexual expression outside marriage is wrong. And while Jesus taught us to come aside and rest, laziness and excessive indulgence in the comforts and luxuries of a life of ease are against God's will. The average man in this world surrenders to his flesh too much. If a person is really repentant, his desires to indulge in these lusts will change.

The Lust of the Eyes

This is covetousness, which is practiced around the world both by those who have very little and those who have very much. To be covetous is to be possession-oriented. The problem with this is that it tends to lessen our desires to be people-oriented, and so keeps us further from the will of God.

Covetousness is a part of the world system which we as Christians are to resist. Jesus spoke up loudly on this issue when He said, "A man's life does not consist in the abundance of his possessions" (Luke 12:15). As far as God is concerned, success is not measured in possessions. Godly wealth is walking closely with the Lord and with those around us (I Timothy 6:18-19). We must preach this message by our lifestyle.

The Pride of Life

Simply stated, this is the desire to be worshiped. Most of us would never admit to thinking like that, but even so, we must constantly resist the desire to elevate ourselves. This is what led the devil astray (Isaiah 14:12-15), and it is what led the Pharisees from the true path during the time of Christ (John 5:44). It has also been the reason why respected church leaders have fallen.

The pride of life may be expressed in such non-obvious ways as criticizing someone else so our efforts look better. It is totally opposed to the way of humble trust in which Jesus intends us to live. For many people, the lust for power, public esteem, and prestige is even more compelling than the lust for money or sexual immorality.

Turn from Ourselves

The apostle Paul points out that Jesus Christ died so that we should no longer live for ourselves, but live for Him who died for us (II Corinthians 5:15). Not to respond to Christ's sacrificial love is to be monstrously ungrateful (Luke 14:26; Romans 14:9).

Turn from the Devil

According to Ephesians 2:2, we were all followers of the devil until we came to Christ. The apostle John emphasized this concept when he wrote that he who is sinful is of the devil (I John 3:8). Some people will not feel they have been consciously living for the evil one, but at the moment of their repentance, they should realize how much they have served Satan's purposes by not living for God.

Obviously, those who have dealt in black magic, witchcraft, and sorcery will be more aware of how they have been in the devil's kingdom. They need to clearly understand that Jesus Christ has power over Satan, and that Christ came specifically to destroy his works (Colossians 2:15; Hebrews 2:14; 1 John 3:8).

I once struck up a conversation at a Teen Challenge center with a young man dressed in a black leather jacket. He told me that he had been involved in black magic, and was reluctant to receive Christ. He told me that the devil had warned him that if he ever turned to God, satanic forces would be after him.

In turn, I told him about Scriptures showing that Christ's power is superior to the devil's (Colossians 2:15; Hebrews 2:14), and he was relieved to know that Christ's power was greater. He confessed his sin of black magic, and I rebuked the evil one. He sat there awestruck. After a while, he testified that he felt like his heart could just burst with happiness! Such was his deliverance from the fear of the devil.

Turn from Idols

The Old Testament is full of God's commandments about not worshiping idols. The Bible laments the fact that people would deny worship due to the Creator of the universe by bowing before images made of gold, silver, or stones (Deuteronomy 7:25-26; I Thessalonians 1:9; Acts 17:24-25). In the New Testament, idolatry is one of those sins which, if found in a person's life, would prevent their entrance into the Kingdom of God (Galatians 5:19-21; I Corinthians 6:9-10; Revelation 21:8).

Many Christians are reluctant to say anything against idols. I'm not suggesting that you speak out against them during the early stages of your witnessing conversation. However, I believe that if a person indicates a desire to be saved, we should mention the need to forsake idols before praying for him. Otherwise, it has the potential of leading to all sorts of frustrations at a later date.

According to Scripture, real salvation cannot occur if the person does not turn from idolatry (Revelation 21:8). But I think we should also remember this: anything that completely consumes our time and energy—like a car, a girlfriend, or even a hobby—can be just as much an idol as a statue made of brass!

By waiting until our friend has come this far in his understanding of the Gospel, he should now understand the necessity of forsaking idol worship. The apostle Paul had words of approval for the Christians of Thessalonica when he wrote, "You turned to God from *idols* to serve the living and true God, and to wait for his Son from heaven..." (I Thessalonians 1:9-10, italics mine).

Those who have been habitual idol worshipers should be told

that the devil often gives power to those idols they worshiped. That is all part of his scheme to keep people in the deceptive bondage of idolatry. Those coming to Christ need to know their authority in the Lord to be able to withstand any attack of the devil (Colossians 2:15; Hebrews 2:14). But Satan will only flee from their rebuke after they have repented and destroyed their idols.

Repentance in this area can be costly. When the Ephesians forsook their black magic, the value of the books they burned was the equivalent of 50,000 days' wages—almost 7 years' wages for 20 men (Acts 19:19)! Those who come to Christ today must destroy their statues, too. These idols must not be sold or given to others, no matter how much they are worth. That would only perpetrate the evil practice from which all are commanded to turn. The biblical pattern is to burn idols (Deuteronomy 7:5,25).

The worshiping of ancestors comes into the category of idolatry, as well. It is wrong for man to worship sinful man (Acts 10:25-26; 14:12-15). Even if an angel were to visit us, we would be forbidden to worship him (Revelation 19:10). If we are not allowed to worship God's perfect angelic creation, how much less is man fit to be given homage?

The above instruction needs to be given with considerable gentleness, because it is not always easy for someone to drop the beliefs of a lifetime in just five minutes. In Chinese culture, for example, age is held in such great respect that it is easy to understand how they could begin to worship their ancestors over a period of time. A Chinese man once told me that his ancestors long ago were believers in the one true God, and they correctly worshiped their fathers' God. But later on, they began to worship their fathers' gods. Then it degenerated further until they worshiped their fathers.

We must state the truth against ancestor worship in such a sensitive way that we do not attack the highly commendable practice of respecting one's elders. We must make sure that our listeners don't believe that our instruction is merely an extension of the disrespectful way in which many Westerners treat their elderly. Non-Westerners won't be so accepting of our teaching if we don't respect our elders.

The Bible commands us all to honor our parents, and Paul instructed the Ephesians to care for family members, telling them that repaying parents and grandparents was pleasing to God (I Timothy 5:4). But we must teach the difference between godly respect and ungodly worship.

We may need to warn those who renounce ancestral worship of the possibility of Satan's attacks. But they also need to be assured that Christ's power is supreme over everything as they submit to Him (James 4:7).

Turn from Our Careers When Necessary

We all know that Saul of Tarsus was a Jewish rabbi who persecuted Christians and consented to their executions. In his own words, he was once "a blasphemer and a persecutor and a violent man" (I Timothy 1:13). Once he became a Christian, Saul could not continue in the religious system in which he found himself. This meant giving up a career for which he had trained many years, and it meant going against the stream of opinion within his culture.

Since we're told that Pharisees loved money, Paul also had to be willing to give up a comfortable lifestyle (Luke 16:14). We do know that Paul turned his back on the career which had earlier brought him honor, and turned his attention to the preaching of the Gospel. This new vocation sometimes brought him opposition, humiliation, and suffering, but he became the much-loved apostle Paul, a man who has affected the world for Christ probably more than any other during the history of the Church.

Moses is another good example of someone who gave up a career for the Lord. Although at one time he enjoyed the pleasures and luxuries of a palatial home in Egypt, the Bible tells us that Moses chose to suffer abuse with the children of God rather than to enjoy the pleasures of sin for a season (Hebrews 11:25). What was his sin? The riches he was enjoying were the result of oppression. Pharaoh had forced the Hebrew people to labor in cruel conditions, and Moses lived on the profits of their slavery. This implied that he agreed with this oppression, so he left that lifestyle.

Billy Graham has told the story of a man who owned a liquor

store who came to an evangelistic meeting and turned his life over to Christ. The next day, this man put up a notice outside his business which read, "Out of Business." Throughout history, many people changed their occupations when they met Jesus.

Repentance means the immediate linking of ourselves with the purposes of God. How different this kind of repentance is from many of the decisions that are registered for Christ today. I pray that this book will encourage Christians to lead those to Christ who will be like Caleb, who "followed the Lord wholeheartedly" (Deuteronomy 1:36).

Make Restitution Where Necessary

We must never forget that the sacrifice of Jesus Christ on the cross provides the way back to God. But even so, God requires us to put right what we can, thus being reconciled to those whom we have hurt. Zacchaeus showed his repentance when he said he would give half of his goods to the poor, and that if he had robbed anyone, he would restore it fourfold (Luke 19:8). The Bible teaches that we should pay back what we have stolen (Leviticus 6:4-5; Ezekiel 33:15; Matthew 3:8; Acts 26:20).

I can remember quite clearly the things I stole during my unsaved era—cigarettes, cookies, chocolate bars, socks, books, and so on. I can also remember the letters of restitution I wrote during Bible college days, and the checks I enclosed.

I addressed one envelope containing both a check and an apology for lying to the store owner, who had suspected I had stolen a particular book. And I can still remember going with check in hand to the manager of Woolworth. For some reason, I had felt before God that I was not to send it through the mail, but to go in person—probably because it was in that particular store that I had been caught stealing as a twelve year old.

We must remember that we cannot always make restitution for the things and lives we have damaged. How can a young man pay back the virginity he has robbed from a young lady? Obviously, there are some things we cannot repay. But even in such circumstances, it would be fitting for the young man to deeply acknowledge his wrong and make sure that any illegitimate child is being properly supported and prayed for.

Not only does a Christian want to undo the damage that Satan is presently causing, but he also wants to undo any damage he helped the devil do through his life before he came to Christ.

When things have become too cloudy to trace, we can always appeal to God for wisdom (James 1:5). God will tell us what we should do. Don't try to rack your brain to remember every little detail—God will bring things to your attention, and you must take care of those. Where details are hazy, He can always ask you to do something to show your willingness to put that thing right. But be prepared to humble yourself. And who knows? They might forgive you—in that case, you're free, and will not have to repay.

When I went back to Woolworth, the manager would not accept my check. But in that particular instance, I didn't really feel that he was forgiving me from a righteous base. He said that the reason he would not receive my money was that he had stolen things when he was a boy! So I went around the corner and gave the money to a Christian organization—an action inspired by Numbers 5:7-8. But that was my conviction; God may convict you to do something quite different.

I am reminded of the story of a young man I'll call Jack. He was a boat builder who was witnessing to his boss, but stealing special copper nails from him at the same time! One day, Jack's pastor preached a message on restitution. Jack was convicted. *My boss will think I am a hypocrite if I confess and put that right,* he thought, *but I know what I must do.* The young man put the matter right.

Jack's boss was touched. "I had considered you a hypocrite, but now, I'm not sure." He went on to say that any religion which moves someone to put a matter like this right is worth looking into! Of course, we make restitution to put things right with those we've offended, and not to preach. Yet it's interesting how often this act of obedience makes people sit up and think seriously about the Lord. After all, it's a more powerful communicator than a sermon on the justice of God. That's because people are experiencing the justice of God as they receive what was stolen from them.

The Bible teaches that repentance should be proved by the lives that we lead (Matthew 3:8; Acts 26:20). Making restitution is a tangible proof of the kind of repentance that God has in mind for us to practice.

John the Baptist indicated another way—the way of generosity—in Luke 3:8-14: "The man with two tunics should share with him who has none, and the one who has food should do the same." He then proceeded to tell the tax gatherers that they would prove their repentance by forsaking corruption, "Don't collect any more than you are required to." Finally, he instructed the soldiers to show their repentance by forsaking violence and being just. But he also added another proof of repentance: he told them to be content with their pay! I wonder if Pontius Pilate, the Roman Governor, heard how his soldiers were being instructed? He'd have been quite impressed if he had.

As we come to the end of this discussion of repentance, remember that not everything mentioned here needs to be said to the person interested in salvation. But we must be careful about the manner in which we say these things. If we sound cold, like an unsympathetic magistrate, we will only testify against the goodness of God.

God's commandments are not burdensome (I John 5:3). But we must not go to the other extreme, bringing God's justice into question by portraying Him as sentimentally soft. God is gentle, as we have already seen. But He still wants "rug-thumping" repentance. That's a deeper kind of repentance than is generally practiced today.

13

Other Things We Must Do

Having dealt with the subject of repentance, let's look at the other things a serious inquirer should consider before committing his life to Christ.

Believe that Jesus is the Only Way

If you have been witnessing to someone using the suggestions in this book, you have come to the stage where your friend needs to acknowledge that only Christ is Lord. For reasons we have already seen, this is going to be tough for those who have been steeped in New Age thought or Hinduism. *Acknowledging Jesus as Lord, to the exclusion of all others,* will prove their readiness to embrace Christianity.

This particular belief puts us on a collision course with many people, upsetting them very much. In many cases, it's inevitable. But I also think we sometimes alienate people unnecessarily by "throwing our pearls before pigs," as we saw earlier. It might be wise to only talk about the exclusiveness of Christ with those who are seriously interested in becoming Christians.

Even so, you might still be asked: "Aren't you being selfish to believe that Jesus is the only way to heaven? What about Buddha, Confucius, Muhammed, and others?" In answer, you might invite them to compare these religious leaders with Christ, and see if we are indeed being unreasonable.

The first question you might wish to politely ask is, "Did any of them claim to be God?" We know Buddha did not, because he wasn't sure there even was a God. Muhammed didn't claim to be God. In fact, Muhammed would have been very indignant if anyone had asked him if he were deity. To him, Allah alone was God.

Second, you might ask, "Did any of these leaders forgive sin?"

I am not aware that any of them claimed to cleanse guilty people from their wrongdoing. Third, ask, "Did any of them rise from the dead?" The answer, of course, is no, they didn't even claim to. But we have solid proof—the kind of proof that would stand up in court—that Jesus did rise from the dead.

Fourth, you could even consider, under some circumstances, courteously asking, "Did the leaders of the other world religions radically change lives for the better?" For every 100 prostitutes that Jesus Christ cleanses, for example, how many Buddhists undergo this kind of change? For every 100 homosexuals or drug addicts whom Christ changes, I wonder how many have been made new through the teachings of Confucius (or even Ram or Krishna)? And for every 100 murderers changed by Christ, how many are changed by following the other leaders?

Two and two equals four, and every day the tides go in and out. We are not being unreasonable to believe these proven facts. In the same way, we are not being selfish or unreasonable to believe that only Jesus is the way to God, and that forgiveness is found in Him alone. A belief in facts also leads us to intelligently follow Jesus Christ, the Son of the living God.

The Scripture is firm on this issue. Jesus said, "No one comes to the Father *except through me*" (John 14:6, italics mine). The apostle Peter put it this way: "Salvation is found in no one else, for there is *no other name* under heaven given to men by which we must be saved" (Acts 4:12, italics mine). And the apostle Paul declared, "For there is one God and *one* mediator between God and men, the man Christ Jesus" (I Timothy 2:5, italics mine).

While we must be uncompromising in our beliefs, it is essential that our spirits exhibit the character of Christ as we share these truths in the proper time. Facts must be expressed in a way that is consistent with the love and spirit of the Son of God. Otherwise, it will be harder for our words to be owned by the Holy Spirit, whose job it is to lead men into all truth (John 16:13). If our words are not said in the right way, our uncompromising stance will be perceived as arrogance. Once that happens, we run the risk of losing our audience, and potentially losing their loving commitment to Christ.

Make Jesus Lord

Submission to the lordship of Christ is actually a natural outgrowth of having been lovingly wooed by Him. It should be reasonable to think that because of Jesus Christ's staggering sacrifice for us, we would want to respond by throwing ourselves at His feet. Not that Jesus requires this for selfish reasons. He is thinking of our good and of the welfare of the whole universe.

The most sensible thing we can do with our lives is to let Him guide and shape them. Paul's words, "And He died for all, that those who live should no longer live for themselves but for him who died for them and was raised again," mean that making Jesus the Lord of our lives is not optional (II Corinthians 5:15).

Witness for Christ

In the gospels, Jesus taught that salvation is conditional upon taking a stand for Him, for He said, "Whoever acknowledges me before men, I will also acknowledge him before my Father in heaven. But whoever disowns me before men, I will disown him before my Father in heaven" (Matthew 10:32-33).

We have been told to preach the Gospel as well as letting our lives speak (Matthew 5:16). If Jesus said that the mouth speaks out of the overflow of the heart (Matthew 12:34), then the proof of our hearts' conversion will find expression through our lips.

Paul's words, "If you confess with your mouth, 'Jesus is Lord,'...you will be saved" (Romans 10:9-10), are extremely important to understanding this point. When these words are placed in their cultural context, they reinforce even further the need for being counted for Christ.

Paul was writing to people in Rome, where Caesar worship was practiced. Believers were confronted sometimes by Roman officials who demanded that they say, "Caesar is Lord," or they would lose their lives. Paul's words left no room for doubt. The one who said, "Jesus is Lord" in those circumstances would be saved.

That's a far cry from mumbling that Jesus is Lord (with perhaps no intention of repentance) at some altar call in the safety of a church.

Continue On for the Lord

To really understand this concept, we must go back to the definition of salvation—knowing and loving God. It's unthinkable to believe that salvation could be maintained indefinitely without a continued walk with the Lord. That would defeat the whole purpose of salvation. It would also devalue the painful work of the Cross, which paved the way for man's salvation.

God would not want any of us to give up after we have started in our walk for Him. With this in mind, let's look carefully at this condition, spelled out for us by Paul: "But now he has reconciled you...to present you holy in his sight, without blemish and free from accusation—*if you continue in your faith,* established and firm, not moved from the hope held out in the gospel" (Colossians 1:22-23, italics mine).

Many fail to see the justice of God here. But to me, it seems quite understandable. If a man trusts Christ and turns from his former evil, all is forgotten. We all agree with that. If God is just—and we know He is—then the reverse must also be true. That is, if a man forsakes his former righteousness, that righteousness will no longer be counted. And that is exactly what the Bible says: "If a righteous man turns from his righteousness....none of the righteous things he has done will be remembered" (Ezekiel 18:24).

The above verses stress man's accountability, and have been put into the Bible for a purpose. But God doesn't leave us unaided. He is always there—loving, helping, and wanting us to do well. It would be wise to also share with your listener such verses as, "He who began a good work in you will carry it on to completion until the day of Christ Jesus" (Philippians 1:6), and "[He] is able to keep you from falling and to present you before his glorious presence without fault and *with great joy*" (Jude 24, italics mine).

This concludes our discussion on repentance and the other conditions necessary for salvation. Remember, we need not go into all these details in our conversations, but these have been given mainly for our understanding. However, it is important that we mention the essence of this teaching, and if we have, the inquirer should be in a position to pray.

Unless God has done extraordinary preparation in someone's life, I believe we should allow the inquirer a day or two to think over everything involved in salvation before committing himself to such a drastic change of lifestyle. If we are going to err in the timing of the sinner's prayer, I feel it is better to err on the side of caution rather than to urge a person into making a rash decision.

When we lead someone to the Lord, we are taking him along an entirely different road from the one he's been on. He'll have to have new and godly ambitions with new friends. He may acquire enemies—even members of his own household (Matthew 10:36). If we do not lay the proper foundation, he may have second thoughts at a later stage.

For anyone who does want to follow Christ, it is good if he prays his own prayer aloud. This step will mean much more to him if he does. The ideal is to provide an opportunity, in an atmosphere of love, for the Holy Spirit to bring such conviction that the sinner spontaneously cries out to God. The reality of Jesus' death on the cross provides an opportunity for this kind of response.

When researching a doctrine of special interest, Bible scholars usually look for the first reference in the Bible to that doctrine. This reference usually gives foundational information on the doctrine. For this reason, Acts 2:14-36 merits attention, because it is the first time we read of the disciples preaching the Gospel after receiving the Great Commission. The reaction of those hearing their preaching should also be of interest to us. Under the convicting power of the Holy Spirit, they cried aloud, "What shall we do?" (Acts 2:37). That sounds like they were ready to be prayed for!

Later in the book of Acts, we read of the Philippian jailor who got down on his knees and also cried, "What must I do to be saved?" (Acts 16:30).

The experience of C.H. Spurgeon is noteworthy, as well. When Spurgeon was fourteen, the Holy Spirit came upon him in convicting power, even though he had been a moral person. He was not like many other boys his age who were dishonest, untrustworthy, and profane. Yet on that particular day, Spurgeon saw how outrageous his sin was against God. Seeing the majesty of the Lord contrasted with his sinfulness filled him with penitence. There is no doubt about one thing: A person's lasting spiritual life will only go as deep as his brokenness over sin goes (Matthew 23:12).

That was certainly true in Spurgeon's life. Just five years after those deep dealings, Spurgeon was preaching to crowds of 5,000 at the age of nineteen. His critics said that he would burn out and drop like a falling star. But he didn't. He continued to serve God faithfully, and became known as "the prince of preachers," leading many to righteousness. It is interesting to note that he gave no "altar calls," but simply told his audiences that he would be in his study if anyone wanted to talk to him.

So far, we have been mentioning conversions that took place without any hint of a plea to "come forward" by a persuasive evangelist. In fact, altar calls were unheard of until Charles Finney introduced them in the 1800s. But then Finney gave people the opportunity to respond to these calls *only after they had been under conviction for days, if not weeks!*

Deep dealings with God produce results. Finney had lasting fruit from his "slow" methods of evangelism. I am told that after his meetings in Rochester, New York, a total of 100,000 people came to the Lord. Ten years later, eighty percent of those converts were still standing firm, and the bars and drinking saloons in the community were still closed. The challenge is always this: How do we provide the Holy Spirit the opportunity to bring conviction in an atmosphere of love, not condemnation? That's a question we each have to wrestle with.

There will be those times when you'll feel the need to give instruction on how someone coming to Christ should pray. In these cases, you could possibly give them the following guidelines on what to tell God at this important moment:

- They have willfully done wrong to hurt Him and others.
- They will turn from everything they know is wrong, and ask His forgiveness.

- They will ask for His grace to overcome the power of sin in their lives.
- They submit themselves to the Lordship of Christ, and take sides with Him to fight against evil in the world.
- They will read the Bible, pray, fellowship with other Christians, and testify about our Lord Jesus Christ.

At other times, you may even feel the need to lead someone in prayer. That is, you pray first, then allow that repentant person to follow you in prayer, sentence by sentence. If you do this, linger with your head bowed before you say "Amen," praying silently that God would confirm things to the person who has just prayed. This is a hallowed moment, and is sometimes spoiled by immediate talk. Allow the Holy Spirit to speak to the new Christian's heart, bringing assurance, instruction, and even further conviction.

Even if you do not lead the person to Christ, I suggest that you ask to pray with him before you leave. Obviously you will not pray the sinner's prayer, but you can pray that God would increase his understanding of what you've been telling him.

After prayer, apply the same method of allowing God to speak to his heart by the Holy Spirit. It is interesting to note that when you lift your head with the "Amen" (after lingering just a little), you'll often notice the person wiping away a tear. That's because he's been touched by God's Spirit—perhaps for the first time in his life. This may be because you have been the first person he has ever heard pray who is in communion with God. His heart will be softer the next time you, or someone else, visits him.

This reminds me of a time some years ago when I was returning home to Hawaii from a trip to Asia. As I took a taxi to Hong Kong's Kai Tak Airport, I excitedly prayed for the person God was going to put me beside on my next flight, which would take me to Manila.

When I boarded the flight, I discovered that my assigned seat was beside the aisle, and there were only two seats in that row, which was ideal for a witnessing situation. Seated by the window was a young lady from the Philippines. As I took my seat, we started talking, and I found out that she was from Baguio, the city in the Philippines where Margaret and I had lived for ten happy years.

As the conversation continued, I learned that Juanita was fleeing from a cruel employer. She was fearful, wondering how her parents would react to her sudden reappearance. They had helped pay for her trip to Hong Kong to find a job. In God's perfect timing, He had placed me in a position to help lessen her fears. Although we enjoyed a good time of talking together, and she listened to my presentation of the Gospel, she didn't give me the impression that she wanted to give her life over to God. So before the plane landed, I simply asked if I could pray with her. She said "yes," and I prayed a very general prayer for her.

Two years later, I received a letter from Juanita. She mentioned how I "led her to Christ" on that Philippine Airlines flight. She now lived in the Middle East, and was asking for tracts to distribute!

I puzzled over that for a couple of months until a friend shared the following: "We come to Christ," he said, "when we say 'yes' to God, not when we pray a sinner's prayer." That really makes sense. But then so does the opposite thought: How many people do we pray the sinner's prayer with—and yet they never say "yes" to God in their hearts?

So by all means, pray a general prayer about God leading your listener into truth, about increasing his understanding of the things you have shared, about helping him turn away from what he knows is wrong, about blessing his family, and about healing him. Although he may never pray after you, he may well be saying "yes" to God—at least in the sense that he'll start doing some serious thinking about what you've shared. This is a very good reason why we should revisit interested contacts.

14

Counting the Cost

It is possible that even after having read the foregoing chapters you may well say to yourself, *I don't think we have to be all that careful before we lead people in a sinner's prayer.* I can certainly understand why you feel that way. Perhaps if we examine Jesus' discourse in Luke 14:25-35, it will shed further light on the subject.

These verses tell of the day when Jesus addressed a large crowd. Although we know that the Lord wants all people to be saved (I Timothy 2:4; II Peter 3:9), it appears that He wanted to emphasize that He has standards. Let's look at the first point in His sermon on discipleship.

> If anyone comes to me and does not hate his father and mother, his wife and children, his brothers and sisters—yes, even his own life—he cannot be my disciple (Luke 14:26).

The use of a contrast to indicate a comparison is a Hebrew way of teaching, and must be interpreted within that cultural context. Jesus was simply saying, "Anyone who loves his father or mother more than me is not worthy of me; anyone who loves his son or daughter more than me is not worthy of me" (Matthew 10:37).

We are to love our families, of course, for this is godly (Exodus 20:12; Ephesians 5:25; 6:4). But when there is a clash of loyalties between your family and God, Jesus said that we must put Him first.

We must be sensitive and loving when we point this out to non-Westerners who have strong family ties. On the day of judgment, we will appear before God, not our relatives. Loving God more than family, however, was only one part of the commitment Jesus said that He wanted from His listeners.

> And anyone who does not carry his cross and follow me cannot be my disciple (Luke 14:27).

When Jesus said these words, He was again speaking within a specific cultural setting—that of Palestine during Roman times. Anyone carrying a cross had been given the death sentence by crucifixion. Hundreds were put to death in this way.

Therefore, "to carry a cross" meant that one was dead to pride and personal ambition. It meant receiving insults and sneers. But even more important, it meant that if you followed Jesus, you had to be prepared to follow Him even to death. Otherwise, our Savior tells us, "you cannot be my disciple." If Jesus were here in America today, He would have to say, "Unless you are prepared to be put to death by the electric chair or by a lethal injection for following Me, you cannot be My disciple."

Jesus did not recruit by giving just the positive benefits of following Him. He was honest. We need to remember His example and not promise "the moon" to a potential convert. While joy and forgiveness will be given to any repentant sinner, the promise that no more problems will come his way is simply not true. Actually, people are likely to have extra difficulties in some areas because they will now be a threat to the kingdom of darkness!

Many times we are tempted to think that we need to hide the fact that certain sacrifices will be required of a would-be convert. We are afraid that he might not come to the Lord if he knows too much. But I remember making the following observation many years ago while living in Baguio City.

Our YWAM team had been witnessing among the people in the park one day, and they'd invited folks to hear me speak that night. I had chosen as my sermon the conversion story of Zacchaeus, which talks about restitution. Unknown to me, one of our team members had brought a former gang leader named Archie to the meeting. We found out later that Archie and his companions had stolen frequently. One of their pastimes had been to smash car windows and steal the stereo equipment from inside those cars.

One night, Archie and his companions had broken into a

department store and stolen merchandise which they later resold. With their profits, they'd thrown a big party. You would think the message on Zacchaeus and the subject of paying back what you'd stolen would be the last thing that would attract a gang leader to the Gospel!

But Archie came back for more, and heard me speak on yet another occasion. The team member who had first contacted Archie continued to befriend him, and Archie eventually came to the Lord.

Later, I shared this story with Loren Cunningham, the founder and president of Youth With A Mission. I expressed my surprise that a gang leader who had so much to put right would respond to a message on restitution so readily. Loren didn't seem amazed at all. I remember his reply. "Archie felt guilty, and you gave him the opportunity to come out from beneath that load. That's why he responded."

Archie meant business with the Lord. He moved into the YWAM house and joined us in many of our activities. Whenever he could, he worked for the day recording the comings and going of a group of Baguio's jeeps that were used for public transportation. Archie faithfully brought home the pesos he earned, and voluntarily gave a portion of his pay to one of our team members, who in turn kept it safe in an old sock in the cupboard. When Archie had saved enough to pay back someone he had wronged, he made the necessary restitution.

Archie is now with the Lord, having lost his life in a swimming accident while on a Christian outreach. The reason I told you his story is that even though Archie knew he would be required to pay back what he had stolen, this did not keep him from coming to the Lord.

I also believe it is honest to give people time to think about what is involved in becoming a Christian. Jesus implied this by the story He gave to the crowds one day.

"Suppose one of you wants to build a tower," Jesus said. "Will he not first sit down and estimate the cost to see if he has enough to complete it?" (Luke 14:28). Likewise, a person coming to Christ needs to sit down and contemplate: "Once I become a Christian, am I going to continue walking with God despite the cost involved?" I believe that we, as evangelists, need to give people the opportunity to think these things through.

After telling the story about building a tower, Jesus then felt it necessary to reinforce His teaching by giving yet another illustration—this time about a king wanting to go to war with only half the number of troops that the opposing army had. This reminds me of the time Margaret and I heard John Stott, the noted British author on evangelism, speak on this very verse. I am indebted to him for his explanation of this whole passage (Luke 14:25-35), which gave me the inspiration to write this chapter.

Stott quoted Jesus' question concerning the king with troops numbering half of those of his enemies: "Will he not first sit down and consider whether he is able...?" And then Rev. Stott stated that in both stories, there was a common thread. In both instances, the person faced with a decision sat down first to think about what he would do (Luke 14:28,31). Only after that did he go into action. I believe we must allow our contacts to do the same.

But Jesus gave one more aspect about the second story that we should consider. Jesus wanted to emphasize that when we become Christians, we will be "swimming against the current." Would-be converts need to be aware of this when they make their decision.

In one of John Stott's meetings, he gave the audience the opportunity to become Christians in what I consider a thoroughly appropriate manner. He announced that those who wanted to come to Christ were to come to the front to talk to him. But he said he would be dismissing the meeting first.

Then Stott said something like, "You will have to fight against the flow of the crowd to reach me. That will be a good introduction to how it will be when you become a Christian. You'll be fighting against the tide the rest of your life!"

I certainly appreciated Stott's sentiments. After all, people want to know what's ahead of them before they sign up for a job, build a house, or agree to buy a new car. And they feel terribly cheated if information is withheld from them.

Let's not be afraid to let people know the terms of discipleship which Jesus laid down. Actually, I believe one of the reasons why some people don't follow the Lord is because we do withhold information about the terms of discipleship. As a result, the sinner says, "That's too easy!" And I believe he is right!

Just a word of caution. People are willing to accept the conditions of the Gospel if they are presented in a loving way by a person they feel they can trust. But if we appear dogmatic and legalistic, they will not be attracted to Christ, for we will not be exhibiting the character of God. The terms on which Jesus accepts the sinner are not the easiest—the Bible doesn't promise that. They are, however, the very best that God could offer. In fact, the angels are awed by what has been given into our hands (I Peter 1:10-12).

So let's make sure that we state all the above terms in the most Christlike spirit possible.

Section III

Preserving the Results

15

Follow-up

Following up those who have come to Christ can be the most rewarding and exciting aspect of evangelism. Seeing a new Christian making strides to live a life of holiness and tell others about Christ is thrilling.

However, some of us may remember our experiences in follow-up as frustrating and unrewarding. This can often be the case if you didn't make sure that the inquirer was fully ready to come to Christ in the first place. Unless you clearly explained Jesus' terms of discipleship, it's possible that when you visit the new Christian, you may find that he is no longer interested. Unfortunately, this heartbreaking experience is prevalent after many evangelistic campaigns.

Even when you are careful to do things correctly, the need for follow-up still exists. The new Christian often needs much guidance, encouragement, and even protection in some locations. In homes hostile to Christianity, conversion can mean total rejection and persecution, even by members of the new Christian's immediate family. To escape people wanting to kill him, the apostle Paul was smuggled out of a city in a basket in the dead of night soon after his conversion (Acts 9:23-25).

If you're working in developing nations, remember that the people are group-oriented, and will not find it easy to survive spiritually by themselves. They will need to belong to a new group—the loving body of Christ—in a tangible small-group setting. Ideally, they will need the security of knowing that this group will continue to exist for a long time. (Chapter 17 gives more information on non-Western culture.)

Even in a peaceful, non-persecution Western setting, the need for follow-up remains. Let's look at the ministries of two outstanding preachers of the 1700s to illustrate just what I mean. John Wesley, the well-known English evangelist, organized his converts into societies, and appointed leaders over them so they would be adequately instructed and cared for.

On the other hand, George Whitfield, another evangelist in England at that time, had no such follow-up plan. But he was a man of considerable anointing, who moved people by the power of his preaching. On one occasion, he spoke to a crowd of 30,000 from the steps of a windmill without the aid of a microphone. Coal miners with sooty faces wept, their tears leaving tracks down their blackened cheeks.

But just before Whitfield's death, he felt that he had not done enough. He reportedly made the comment that in comparison with the lasting fruit of John Wesley's ministry, he had merely "knitted a rope of sand." That's an important statement. Not all evangelists are called to form a denomination, as John Wesley did. Even so, Whitfield obviously felt that his work was insufficient in organizing follow-up plans for his converts or in making better provision for that process.

In the Bible, the apostle Paul gave some guidelines about this subject. He encouraged the Thessalonians that the lasting fruit of their labor was their reward. He called those whom he had led to Christ, the crown in which he would glory (I Thessalonians 2:19, NKJV). When Paul coined this term, he was thinking of the trophy that victorious athletes received at the ancient Olympic Games.

We would do well to reflect for a moment on this. If Jesus Christ were to return to earth right now, how many people would be our "crown of rejoicing"? This is quite a thought. Our rejoicing would not have to be confined to those we personally led to the Lord. Everyone coming to Christ does so because many Christians have been involved. It is encouraging to think of the people that we as a group in some way led to the Lord—by our praying, our giving, our lifestyle, or our words.

It's very heartening to see strong converts. Paul also thought so, for he wrote, "For now we really live, since you are standing firm in the Lord" (I Thessalonians 3:8). The healthy spiritual state of the believers comforted him in his trials and affliction. "In all our distress and persecution we were encouraged about you because of your faith" (I Thessalonians 3:7).

The work of the Lord can get discouraging at times. But we know that it is really worthwhile when we think of those whom we helped lead to the Lord who are remaining true to God. This is one of the rewards for taking the slower route in evangelism, rather than the "let's have results quickly" approach.

I believe there are several important ingredients to follow-up. First of all, our motive is all important. If our heart is not in our witnessing, it is unlikely that our hearts will be in doing follow-up, either. To the same degree in which we are faithful in the first aspect of evangelism, we are likely to be effective in the second. It is possible to witness out of a sense of duty, because we want to impress others, or for some other questionable reason. But God wants us to witness because we love Him, and because we love people, too!

Witnessing for the wrong motive is often revealed by the shocking lack of interest in follow-up. Some Christians have never bothered to revisit open-hearted people who could be encouraged to follow the Lord. This is an important part of follow-up. Revisiting those whom God is really speaking to, but who haven't yet come to Christ, can often be the means by which they come to faith.

Sincere, warm, unselfish giving of ourselves is costly. But it should be a mark of every Christian. If we're going to be effective, it is important that we have a heart like the one Paul described. Paul's heartfelt concern for his Thessalonian converts led him to do three things in the realm of follow-up.

Paul Revisited His Converts When He Could

The book of Acts is a testimony to the fact that Paul revisited his converts. His primary motive in undertaking his second missionary journey was to revisit those he and Barnabas had led to Christ on their first trip (Acts 15:36).

During that second journey, Paul preached to the Thessalonians and won a number of them to the Lord. Later, he wanted to revisit them, but was hindered by his hostile opponents who had run him out of town earlier.

But Paul was not the kind of person to just shrug his shoulders and do nothing. He cared deeply for his friends. So when he was unable to return, he sent Timothy to exhort and establish them in their faith (I Thessalonians 3:1-2). His desire was to return personally, and I believe that is our first principle in follow-up. If we cannot go, we should make great efforts to send someone else.

So what do we do at the end of a short-term outreach in the next town or in a neighboring state? How do we visit our great contacts when we may now be miles away? The example of the apostle Paul in the last paragraph is certainly something we should take note of.

But what do we do if we have been on a short-term outreach overseas? It is important to introduce our converts to a permanent, loving group as soon after their conversion as possible. If a strong bond is established with the short-term team, the converts will be torn emotionally when the team leaves. This can be very damaging both to the converts and to the advancement of God's Kingdom in that location.

Because of this, the short-termer must make some difficult sacrifices. Obviously, they will want to spend time with their spiritual children. But we must ensure that the new Christians are more strongly bonded to their new family in Christ than they are to us. Remember, new converts must have personal contact with a group which will be around to care for them long term.

Paul Labored in Prayer for His Converts

The great apostle was not content to have people join Christ's cause, then remain immature. He travailed in prayer that Christ be formed in them (Galatians 4:19). Paul wrote of Epaphras as one who labored fervently in prayer all the time for the Colossian Christians who had been subjected to heresy, that they might be mature and stand firm in the will of God (Colossians 4:12).

A missionary who was working among the Lisu people in the southwestern hill country of China was once forced to leave the tribe due to a war going on in that area. Although he was separated from them geographically, he was not separated in spirit. He prayed for them daily, though he was now working with new people in the lowlands. After two years, the situation changed enough to enable him to visit the Lisu again. He noticed something remarkable—the Lisu believers had grown more spiritually as a result of his prayers, than those with whom he had been working down on the plain!

How do we pray for those who have come to the Lord? We should stand in prayer between them and Satan, resisting his attacks on their minds, and praying that God would help them hate sin and resist temptation. We should pray that they would love His Word and the fellowship of the saints. Naturally, we should pray that they would witness to others.

One person coming to the Lord can often open the door for relatives, friends, and neighbors to get saved, too. This is an extremely important subject, and deserves far more space than we can give it here. Missiologists call it *networking*. When people come to Christ, they immediately have an open door to influence many in that special just-after-conversion time—especially in those places where people live in close proximity to each other. It is not uncommon to see many people come to Christ in a short space of time by this process. We should pray for it, encourage it eagerly, and expect it to happen!

When the woman at the well excitedly ran back to her town, she said, "Come, see a man who told me everything I ever did." Many of her townspeople believed in Jesus as a direct result of the woman's enthusiasm. But it didn't stop there. The locals urged Jesus to stay with them. So Jesus stayed for two days, and the movement grew. Because of Jesus' ministry in the town, "many more became believers" (John 4:29-42).

So we must pray for new converts. But we also need to pray for those dear people we've contacted who have not yet yielded their lives to Christ. Pray that God will bring our words back to their minds, and that they would seek honestly after God.

Unfortunately, a wonderful opportunity for the Gospel is lost when we don't pray for those to whom we have just witnessed.

After a Christian has lovingly shared with an unbeliever, the Holy Spirit has much more to work with than He did before. He can now continue to impress upon them the words which we have spoken, and the love we have shown. But we must pray in love and mercy for them. If we pray with any criticism or loathing in our heart, our prayers won't even rise above the ceiling. But how thrilling it is to see people saved as a result of our prayer (I Corinthians 9:10).

Paul Wrote Letters

Paul's letters to the Thessalonians are a lasting testimony that he sat down and wrote letters to exhort and instruct them. If there had been such things as telephones, fax machines, audio cassettes, or video tapes in his day, he would have used these to encourage and instruct his converts, as well. Actually, it can become costly sending books and tapes. But that's just the outworking of the "sharing our lives" concept which the apostle wrote about (I Thessalonians 2:7-8).

To be an effective witness, and to be successful in the ministry of follow-up, some of our spare time will be used in the rewarding pursuit of being with those new babes in Christ—just as a mother delights in spending time with her newborn child.

In the next chapter, we will discuss the things we should teach new converts on these follow-up visits.

16

Instructions for New Converts

If we who have known the Lord for some time puzzle over certain spiritual issues, think how a newborn Christian must feel. Bearing this in mind, I believe that there are six main areas which we should cover with the new convert immediately. Obviously, he will not retain everything in one day, so you can mention these briefly, and explain more fully on subsequent visits.

The Necessity of Prayer

The heart of Christianity is friendship with God. One of the ways we know we are saved is that we have fellowship with Him. We must encourage our newly converted friends to maintain this communion with God at all costs. When Jesus taught His disciples to pray (Matthew 6:9-13), He gave a pattern that encouraged them to begin their prayer by praising God (as opposed to diving to their knees and immediately presenting their "wish list"). By His words, "Hallowed be your name," Jesus inferred that we should first unhurriedly worship and revere the Lord.

Moving on from a time of worship, Jesus urged His disciples to pray, "Your kingdom come. Your will be done on earth as it is in heaven." By this, He meant that His disciples were to pray for others: for people to be saved, for the faithful to be strengthened, and for righteousness to rule in men's hearts. The new convert should be taught to pray for the salvation of his family, and for those to whom he has witnessed. He should be exhorted to remember his Christian brothers in prayer, as well.

Jesus' pattern of prayer then encouraged the disciple to pray for himself and his needs (his daily food, his clothing, and his shelter). He is also encouraged to pray about his spiritual needs (extending forgiveness to others). I can hardly overemphasize this aspect of the prayer. The lack of a forgiving spirit has spelled spiritual ruin to many who otherwise would have risen to do great things for God and His Kingdom.

If you want your friend to remain in Christ and to be effective, this truth of forgiving others has to be stressed. To keep on forgiving (and forgiving!) is one of the key ways to stay spiritually healthy. It is only logical that if we are going to represent Christ's willingness to forgive the sins of the unsaved, our lives must exhibit this forgiving spirit, too!

Immediately after He finished outlining the whole prayer, Jesus commented on only one aspect of that prayer—the part about forgiving others. This truth is so important that Jesus added by way of reinforcement, "But if you do not forgive men their trespasses, neither will your Father forgive your trespasses" (Matthew 6:15, NKJV). He really wanted this point to hit home.

Notice that in the pattern given thus far, the order of prayer has been God first, others second, and self last. This should be the mark of every Christian. John Stott once said that sin is the reversing of this order. The sinner puts self first, others second (when it suits him), and God last, or not at all.

When Jesus ended the pattern of prayer for His disciples to follow, He used the words, "For Yours is the kingdom and the power and the glory forever. Amen." That certainly is a fitting way to end a time with the Lord.

The Importance of the Bible

Once the new convert has confidence in the authority of the Bible, we should explain how essential it is for his spiritual well-being. He should understand that the Bible is the highest court of appeal for the Christian. In the book of Acts, we have an example of just how this "appeals court" works.

The apostle Paul spoke in a Jewish synagogue in the Macedonian town of Berea during his travels. The Jews were very interested in the apostle's message, but they wanted to check it against the Word of God before committing themselves to follow his teaching. "Now the Bereans...received the message with great eagerness and *examined* the Scriptures every day to see if what Paul said was true" (Acts 17:11-12, italics mine).

We're giving a new convert a valuable tool when we teach him to compare every teaching he hears with the overall tone of the Bible. That's because Scripture must be compared with Scripture. One Scripture might say, "Thus says the Lord," but we must put it into context with the surrounding verses and with the whole message of the Bible. An overall knowledge of the Scriptures is a way of safeguarding us all from ungodly principles, or an unscriptural emphasis on some particular facet of God's truth.

In some cultures, you may find it necessary to show the new Christian the passage in II Timothy 3:15-17, especially the words "from infancy you have known the holy Scriptures...." Some people teach that we cannot understand the Bible even as adults. Yet Paul indicated that Timothy had known the Scriptures from childhood.

Some people also teach that tradition has more authority than the Bible. But Jesus warned that it is possible to make the Word of God ineffective by our tradition (Mark 7:9,13; Matthew 15:3,6)—even though we know that not all tradition is wrong. Jesus strongly endorsed the authority of the Word of God over the authority of tradition. He charged the religious elders of His day with error because they did not know the Scriptures (Matthew 22:29). Jesus gave instruction that the Scriptures should be searched and read avidly (John 5:39).

The Importance of a Holy Life

While in some other religions you may ask deities for special favors without being concerned with holiness, that is certainly not true in Christianity. To walk with Jesus is to "seek first his kingdom and his righteousness" (Matthew 6:33). This is in direct contrast to pagans, whom the Bible describes as running after material things (Matthew 6:31-32) and after ungodly behavior (I Peter 4:3-4).

The need for holiness can hardly be overemphasized. It is the cornerstone of our fellowship with God (Hebrews 12:14), the basis of God hearing our prayers (Psalm 66:18), and our guarantee against becoming deceived (II Thessalonians 2:11-12). The key thought in that last Bible verse is that you will become deceived if you take pleasure in sin. The Christian should pray continually that he will hate sin more, and thus become more conformed to the image of Christ (Romans 8:29).

In his excellent book *My Friend the Bible,* John Sherrill gives us some superb advice on overcoming temptation. He encourages us to memorize verses of Scripture that we can quote to ourselves (or to the devil) during times of temptation. He says that Christians should recognize their areas of weakness, and have appropriate Bible verses ready to quote when those temptations arise. I would highly recommend that you read this book and even give copies to those you lead to Christ. [24]

You should also explain what the new Christian should do if he sins. The apostle John wrote, "If we confess our sins, he is faithful and just and will forgive us our sins and purify us from all unrighteousness" (I John 1:9).

Because Jesus suffered and shed His blood, we can be forgiven. That dynamic truth should do several things for us. It reminds us of the cost of forgiveness, so it keeps us humble before God. But it also inspires us to cast aside our sins, come into God's presence, and ask His forgiveness. We shouldn't wallow around in condemnation—a condition that doesn't help us fight against the evil in the world!

The Importance of Keeping Our Lives Separated for God

If Satan cannot stop someone from coming to Christ, he has a few ideas about how to dilute a new Christian's potential for God. Since the devil has been around for thousands of years, he knows there are at least two strategies that a young, ill-informed convert can fall for. Either way, the devil has weakened that person's potential for God.

One strategy is to tempt the new Christian to get involved in a career or job outside of God's will. God calls many people into all sorts of secular jobs, but you should ask the new convert to make sure that his job is the one suited to his talents and gifts, where he can bring the most glory to God. He should also make sure that it is a job where he will not be asked to compromise his Christian stand.

The other strategy of the devil is to tempt the new Christian to marry the wrong person. I cannot overemphasize the need to give the new convert simple instructions about marriage. Caution him to keep his heart and affections in check, and to wait for God's time and God's best. If he doesn't marry the right spouse, it will be very difficult for him to serve the Lord and to raise his children to be men and women of God. Many men have had to settle for a lesser ministry because they married the wrong person, or else they married too soon.

I believe that instruction about all this is essential. If Christians do not keep their ministry and calling in mind when choosing a marriage partner, they will rob God of His due. I feel that the Scripture, "Seek first his kingdom...and all these things will be given to you as well," also relates to a marriage partner.

What if no suitable person is around? I heard of one young lady who did her missionary training at the YWAM Honolulu base some years ago. "I'm called to Pakistan," she mentioned while on base, "and I'm going there even if I don't get married!" She went off to Pakistan to serve in obedience to the Lord. Once there, she met the son of a missionary who had been raised in that country. They married, and the last I heard, they were serving God in Pakistan.

This young lady's story had a fairy-tale ending, but that cannot always be guaranteed. I have to agree with the sentiments of another young lady who said, "If the right man doesn't come along, I'd rather stay single than marry the wrong guy!" So far, she hasn't married.

The Necessity of Fellowship with Other Christians

As you witness, you will often hear the comment that we can be good Christians without going to church. However, the Bible teaches that once we belong to Christ, we also belong to the body of believers worldwide whom God calls "the Church." It is good to teach the new Christian that he has certain responsibilities to discharge to this body of believers. Each of us has a role to play as we exercise our God-given gifts and callings. Likewise, each Christian has the privilege to receive inspiration, instruction, correction, and the encouragement of fellowship from this body.

In practical terms, much of this takes place within a local group of believers who gather regularly. Whether they meet in a cathedral or a jungle clearing, it makes no difference as far at its legitimacy in God's eyes.

The Bible encourages us, "Let us not give up meeting together, as some are in the habit of doing..." (Hebrews 10:25). But God is not looking for mere attendance. If we have been touched by the sacrifice of Christ on Calvary, we should want to relate to a body of believers in a practical way beyond just warming a pew. "You are the body of Christ," Paul told the Corinthian Christians, "and each one of you is a part of it" (I Corinthians 12:27).

Ideally, the new convert should be part of a group that provides spiritual fellowship, teaching, and leadership. It should be a gathering of believers which practices righteousness, and which has a vision to reach those who are unsaved.

We should have sufficient confidence in our leaders that we will be able in good conscience to fulfill the Scripture, "Obey your leaders and submit to their authority. They keep watch over you as men who must give an account. Obey them so that their work will be a joy, not a burden..." (Hebrews 13:17). But we may not have a gathering near us that answers to the description just given. In these circumstances, God would have us find a fellowship that is as close as possible to this ideal.

The Importance of Witnessing to Others

Teaching a convert about witnessing should be relatively easy if you have led that person to Christ. That's because you have already given him an example of witnessing, and he's enjoying the fruits of it. Example is always the best teacher. If we tell people to do things that we are not doing ourselves, the message they will receive is, "What they say is really not very important."

If you have followed the pattern set down in this book, you will have already explained to the new Christian how confessing Christ to others is a condition of salvation. And if you have been witnessing for the glory of God, there must be a desire in your heart to see the world around you won to Christ. Enlist this new convert in the battle to turn the world to God. Encourage him at every turn, yet guide him, too.

A new convert is often high in zeal, but low on wisdom. If you channel his enthusiasm correctly, you will achieve things you might both be amazed at. Endeavor to go witnessing with this new Christian, and pour into him the truths that you know. Put books into his hands that will help him. Pray and fellowship with him, for in this way you will be both discipling him and multiplying your own ministry.

You may want to give instruction on only one of these points each time you visit. But make sure that you give teaching on these six basic subjects as soon as possible.

Section IV

Other Considerations

17

Cultural Differences

Margaret and I were in downtown Manila, far from the cool air of our home in the mountains, and we were feeling the heat. The streets of Manila were often clogged with jeeps and cars, and today was no exception. We inched our way through congested traffic under the tropical sun for about 20 minutes. Mercifully, we were now on a wide street and were able to move at a speed that allowed the air to swirl around us. To the right stood the huge market where Filipinos buy everything from vegetables to trinkets. Along the edge of this very wide street, bare-backed men wearing rubber slippers pushed carts full of cabbage, cans of water, and blocks of ice.

But as we traveled beside the brown waters of the Pasig River, I began wondering why all the traffic appeared to be coming from the opposite direction. I hadn't remembered seeing any one-way signs. Enjoying the rush of air through the open windows of the jeep, I began to unwind inside. I really did enjoy living in the Philippines. But that time of enjoying my thoughts didn't last long. I suddenly saw a traffic officer signaling me to stop. My heart sank. This must be a one-way street! I pulled over to the side of the road, leaving the engine idling.

"Good afternoon," I offered.

"Excuse me, sir," he said politely, bringing his head down to the open window, "where are you going?"

"Just a couple more blocks," I said with a wave of my arm.

He paused and thought for a moment. "Then drive carefully," he admonished, "This is a one-way street. You might get hit!"

You would never hear a policeman in the West say that! This is only one example of the non-confrontational, accommodating, friendship orientation which is quite strong in the non-Western world. And that's not all. Many other values which are foreign to Westerners predominate and pervade every aspect of these societies. Knowledge of their values is essential before embarking on the exciting adventure of preaching Christ in this segment of the world. I wish I had known these things, when I boarded the S.S. Oronsay to sail for the Philippines for the very first time when I was 19.

Please note that when I use the term *non-Westerner*, I mean those peoples usually living in Asia, Africa, the Pacific Islands, or Latin America. All of these countries are quite different from Western countries in their cultures, whether they are poor or are financially equal to Western countries. Let's look at some major differences in the way Westerners and non-Westerners think.

Usually Not Absolute-oriented

Another way of saying this is that personal considerations are more important to non-Westerners than rules or laws are. Consider the traffic incident just mentioned. Had the officer sent me back the other way, it would have taken twenty minutes of fighting the traffic through choked streets to reach our destination. But with the blessing of the policeman, it only took us minutes to get where we wanted to go. Because the road was very wide at that point, and since push carts go up that street the wrong way, it wasn't that difficult (or dangerous) for me to stay clear of the oncoming traffic. The officer was trying to be helpful. He probably didn't want to embarrass me by saying that I was doing something wrong.

Obviously, the extent to which non-Westerners are not absolute-oriented varies, depending on how far their prevailing religion deviates from the Word of God. The philosophy of Hinduism, for example, is considered the furthest removed from the beliefs of Christianity. So in Hindu areas, the contrast between absolutes and relativity is clearly marked. A man steeped in Hindu philosophy will consider truth to be saying what the other person wants to hear, rather than the actual facts.

Many cultures teach that lying is perfectly fine when protecting life or property. One culture I know of will even excuse lying so that lust can be expressed.

Event-oriented, Not Time-oriented

Most cultures have a tolerance threshold for lateness, although in many Western circles, there is no tolerance at all. In other Western areas, it is a mere five or ten minutes. This flexibility is much greater in certain parts of Asia, Africa, the Pacific Islands, and Latin America.

It is usually culturally permissible in the Philippines, for example, to be 20 to 30 minutes late. But I have been in a part of Indonesia where church members arrived for a service one hour late every time. In some remote parts of the non-Western world, it is very acceptable to arrive two days or even two weeks late!

Many times, this is because transport and communications are scarce or even non-existent. Partly due to being raised this way, and partly because of their orientation to people rather than goals, certain non-Westerners tend to think, "As long as we have the event, so what if it doesn't start on time?"

More Fellowship-oriented Than Goal-oriented

We in the West can learn so much from our non-Western brothers. It is true that we have comfortable standards of living, and we have advanced in technology to conquer outer space. But sometimes I think we haven't conquered in the places where it really counts. When it comes to *inner space,* a non-Westerner usually wins hands down.

Dr. Billy Graham has said that loneliness is the greatest problem in our society. Dr. James Hodge, a professor at Northeastern Ohio University, says, "The major underlying reason is that people are so achievement-oriented, so wrapped up in themselves, so focused on their personal interests that they're unable to make or maintain healthy, close relationships."[25]

What we're seeing today is the results of the "me" generation. The problem has been aggravated by the obsession to succeed, to have material possessions, and to be a winner. We have been successful in these areas. We have our material possessions, but they have come with a fearsome price tag.

In the drive for success, we have alienated people, including even our loved ones. As a result, we are lonely. America has one of the highest rates for teenage suicides in the world with 1,000 attempts a day. [26] We also have one of the highest divorce rates for Christians in the Western world.

True, it is godly to have goals. But it becomes ungodly if those goals isolate us from people and from the flow of emotional energy that comes from being properly related to others.

Many non-Westerners are shining examples to us in this. The non-Westerner loves the company of others. There is always room for one more. In having many non-Westerners on teams I have led over the years, I have found it necessary to allow them time for ample fellowship, fun, and laughter.

During the years I led the YWAM center in Baguio City in the Philippines, I found that I needed to declare a holiday every now and then—even for half a day—so we could sit around, drink coffee, and have fellowship. They all loved that. More than that, they needed those times of interaction in a relaxed atmosphere.

Often Does Not Like to Confront

An important point to remember when working in the non-Western World or among non-Westerners is this: you must never make anyone feel bad about themselves. If you ever need to bring correction to a non-Westerner, it must be done in an uplifting way. If you feel like throwing up your hands and saying, "You can't do that," think of the discussion we've had on how Jesus ministered to the woman at the well, and how He dealt with Zacchaeus.

From childhood, many non-Westerners have been taught not to confront. They are taught to conform, and are discouraged from being unique. They are told not to challenge a person older than themselves, because an older person is always considered to be right. If there is a disagreement, the younger must apologize to the elder, even if the older person is in the wrong! Obviously, we are talking about the culture at large. But even so, it is natural that something of the surrounding culture will always infiltrate the

Church in every society where it is found.

But not all non-Westerners are non-confrontational. Sprinkled around the globe are people groups (especially on the Indian sub-continent and in some Chinese societies) who can be very confrontational—with loud voices! But while I have noticed that they may readily confront strangers who do something wrong at a crowded train station, they may avoid pointing out the faults of those they know personally.

While we in the West find it easier to confront, we need to remember two things. First, not all of us obey the scriptural pattern for confrontation. The Scripture says, "If your brother sins against you, go and show him his fault, *just between the two of you*" (Matthew 18:15, italics mine). That command must be one of the most disobeyed of all. Second, when Westerners address wrongs, we often do it in the wrong spirit, which can even be worse than not confronting at all.

So confrontation is biblical. It is also an important ingredient to a mentally healthy life. But if we do it vindictively, we will wound and maim people emotionally.

We must not forget the admonition of the apostle Paul, who wrote, "Brothers, if someone is caught in a sin, you...should restore him gently. But watch yourself, or you also may be tempted" (Galatians 6:1, italics mine). When a non-Westerner learns to confront, he usually does it beautifully, because he does it so sensitively. We Westerners have so much to learn.

Group-oriented, Not Individualistic

Over the centuries, the non-Westerner has learned that for emotional and financial reasons, as well as physical protection, it is better to be group-oriented. This contrasts sharply with the rugged individualism and obsession with personal rights and freedoms of people in the West—particularly in the United States.

The Westerner needs to understand that group orientation is so ingrained into a non-Westerner that it is impossible for him not to think of others, and that is healthy. We have already caught a glimpse of what a mess the "me" generation has made of our society, with the emphasis on individuality. However, the non-Westerner must recognize that one day, he will stand before the judgment throne of Christ as an individual. Group orientation becomes unhealthy when we bow to things that are against the will of God out of deference to others.

Because of his orientation, the non-Westerner usually cannot work outside the context of a group. So when he comes to the Lord and his original clan rejects him, or when his family are out to kill him because he is leaving his traditional religion, he must join a new group.

But a non-Westerner must also belong to a group, even when the extreme circumstances just described do not exist. Emotionally, socially, and psychologically, the non-Westerner is not equipped for living the Christian life alone.

I believe we make a mistake in developing nations when we win someone to the Lord, have him enjoy our fellowship and the emotional satisfaction of our acceptance, and then leave him by himself when our evangelism tour is over. He needs to be introduced as quickly as possible after his conversion to a church or another long-term Christian group. In this way, he will not have the trauma of being emotionally torn when the short-termers leave. When teams haven't left non-Westerners bonded into a long-term group, negative effects have often been the result.

Expects His Parents (or Leader) to Anticipate His Needs

Although the non-Westerner is required by his culture to accept the fact that his elders are always right, there is a definite trade-off, for he receives something in return. His elders assume certain responsibilities for him—one of them being that they will try to anticipate his needs without being told. This makes it much easier for him to defer to those who are in authority.

Unfortunately, we Westerners don't always realize this. Neither do we always understand that because we are foreigners, we are regarded as elders, or at least older brothers, in some cultures.

If you are ever a leader over a non-Westerner, you must accept that he will have certain expectations. One of these expectations is that you will be sensitive to his needs. And remember, he may not be confrontational. He won't necessarily come tell you all about those needs. He may feel very disappointed when you do not notice them, even if you cannot meet them. Actually, for some strange reason, we all feel helped if someone notices our needs—even if that person is unable to satisfy them, no matter what culture we find ourselves in.

Naturally, there are variations to everything we have discussed here. The extent to which all the foregoing applies depends on the amount of influence a particular people group has received from the religious and philosophical teachings around them, or from the colonial power that formerly governed them. Normally these characteristics mark all non-Western countries around the world.

Whenever we enter a new culture, and observe things we don't understand, we must refrain from saying, "This is crazy." Instead, we should look beyond what we observe, and search for the reason for what we see. It may not be logical to the Western mind. It may not line up scripturally, but usually we can come to an understanding of why things are done the way they are. After all, we are only seeing the tip of the iceberg. The reasons can be buried deep below.

Once we understand why a trait has evolved, we can be compassionate. And when compassion is present, the non-Westerner is released more readily to make the effort to obey the biblical principles which we are trying to expound. When they see our love—not our criticism—they will even overlook (for a time) the most terribly offensive cultural mistakes that we make. And we Westerners all make them.

Obviously, it takes time to learn all these things, but learn them we must. As we recognize the strengths of the non-Western culture, we should also gently point out the strengths of the biblical patterns (but not necessarily the things we like about American or European cultures).

The six characteristics mentioned above are not the only cultural differences that emerge. There are other differences that separate people groups. To the Westerner, achievement can be all important, whereas to others, a sense of belonging is of far greater value. In the same way, there are cultures where money is valued, and there are cultures where it is not. Some cultures regard competition as important, while others disdain it. The differences go on and on! [27]

You may find it a bit of a hassle to have to understand another person's culture, but it's worth the effort, even though you won't comprehend everything overnight. If the people of the culture recognize that you love and enjoy them, they will be your friends for the rest of your life!

18

Is the Bible Inspired?

I have found nine simple reasons why the Bible can be trusted, and why we can place our faith in its teachings. We mentioned previously that some people may desire to prove the Scriptures to be God's Word very early in their conversation with a non-believer. Once the listener is convinced of the Bible's authenticity, it is a powerful tool to use. But it is important for us to realize that simply quoting II Timothy 3:16: "All Scripture is inspired by God...." is not objective proof to the non-Christian of the Bible's divine origin. That proof must come from sources outside the Scriptures. So what proofs can we use?

Although pages could be written on each of the following points, I've included only the basics on each reason we can trust in the inspiration of the Scriptures.

Historical Documents Prove the Bible

The NIV Study Bible lists 39 ancient texts as examples of non-biblical documents from long ago. These 39 texts are merely the major ones which provide information similar to various Old Testament passages, or which shed light on them.

For example, inscriptions were found which vividly describe the desperate days preceding the siege of Jerusalem by Nebuchadnezzar, the Babylonian king in 588-586 B.C.—a siege that was mentioned in Jeremiah 34.[28]

As for the New Testament, the historians Pilo, Eusebius, Josephus, and others, together with Jewish sacred writings, record things parallel to the testimony of the New Testament writers. Historians attest to the accuracy of the list of government and religious rulers in power in Palestine during the fifteenth year of Tiberius Caesar, which is mentioned in detail in Luke 3:1-2.

Archaeology Upholds the Testimony of Scripture

In his book *Rivers in the Desert,* Dr. Nelson Gluech, an outstanding Jewish archaeologist, has made the powerful statement that no archaeological discovery has ever contradicted the Bible. Examples abound of how this science of the study of ancient times confirms biblical statements. Archaeologists have uncovered numerous coins, writings, and city sites which have confirmed the biblical record. For example, they have uncovered evidence of the existence of Lysanias, the Tetrarch of Abilene (Luke 3:1-2). Before this discovery, skeptics had considered Luke's reference to the ruler to be in error.

In 1961, a team of Italians unearthed an important inscription bearing the name of Pontius Pilate as they excavated in Caesarea. The stone calls Pilate "Prefect," which corresponds to Luke's term of "Governor." (Later, Rome's rulers of the Judean province were not called "Governors," but "Procurators.") This discovery again confirms the accuracy of Luke's pen.

Between 1929 and 1936, John Garstang made excavations at the site of Jericho, the first city captured by the incoming Israelites under Joshua (Joshua 6). Garstang found evidence that the city had been destroyed suddenly, because the grain bins were full, and there was plenty of food. He also found evidence from charred remains (and the broken-down walls), that the city had been burned (Joshua 6:24), and that the walls had completely come down (Joshua 6:20).[29] Further examples along these lines can be found in Paul E. Little's book *Know Why You Believe.* [30]

Modern Science Confirms Biblical Statements

Indian sages once taught that the earth was supported by elephants, while the Greeks said that Atlas carried the earth on his back. Yet three thousand years ago, one Bible writer declared: "He suspends the earth over nothing" (Job 26:7). In the sixth century A.D., the geographer Ptolemy numbered the stars at one thousand.

Today, science has confirmed through the aid of powerful telescopes what the prophet said hundreds of years before Christ: "as countless as the stars of the sky" (Jeremiah 33:22). There are passing references in the Word of God about the world being round (Isaiah 40:22), a piece of knowledge that took science thousands of years to catch up on.

For many years, the passage of Scripture, "If those days had not been cut short, no one would survive" (Matthew 24:21-22), seemed absurd. How could there ever come a time when man would be capable of annihilating himself? For even during the Second World War—the most destructive war in history—the population of the world increased faster than the ravages of war could decrease it. An estimated 50 million people were wiped out during that hellish nightmare.

But these days, even with the Cold War over and nuclear bombs being dismantled, thousands of bombs remain. Even one of these could annihilate a city the size of New York or Tokyo. Our stockpiled weapons could wipe everybody off the face of the planet! No longer can it be said that the above Scripture has no meaning.

Modern Medicine Also Confirms Biblical Assertions

Following are two examples that show it was comparatively recently that medical science caught up with what the Bible said through Moses thousands of years ago.

If you were a pregnant woman in a maternity ward during the 1800s, your chances of dying were one in six. This was mainly because of the doctors' practice of not washing their hands between examining dead bodies and performing pelvic examinations among the living.

A young Hungarian doctor at the Vienna General Hospital in Austria—Ignaz Semmelweis—set up a rule that doctors must wash their hands after touching the dead. Many people bitterly opposed him for his ideas, but he persisted in his beliefs.

Three months after this rule came into effect, only one woman had died out of eighty-four. But what Semmelweis wrote in his classic work published in 1861 had already been set forth in Numbers chapter 19, thirty-two centuries before!

Likewise, there used to be time when doctors would let the blood out of sick people as a cure. But today, medical science has realized the error of this practice, confirming what Moses wrote centuries ago, "The life of a creature is in the blood" (Leviticus 17:11). Transfusions of blood are now given on many occasions, because the blood carries the power of life to heal, not to sicken.

These two illustrations are both from *None of These Diseases* by Dr. McMillen. I certainly recommend this book for further examples proving the value of the divine record from a medical viewpoint. [31]

The Bible Confirms What Our Conscience Says About Sin

To me, this is an outstanding reason why it is so easy to place our faith in the Bible as opposed to believing other sacred texts (which sometimes allow certain sins). For what good would holy writings be if they were to advocate murder, lust, greed, rape, and violence? "The law of the Lord is perfect.... The statutes of the Lord are trustworthy..." (Psalm 19:7). We know that the Bible is the Word of God, because its moral teachings have the same law and order as there is in the physical universe—perfect beauty and symmetry. No wonder that Scripture is to be desired more than much fine gold (Psalm 19:10).

Biblical Prophecy Has Been Fulfilled Consistently

The overwhelming number of biblical predictions which have been fulfilled in detail prove that the Bible is the Word of God. It does not take much to be able to predict generalities such as, "One day you will meet a fine young lady and marry her," or to have prophesied that a recession would hit the U.S. some day! Neither is it sufficient to say that the Bible is inspired because of fulfilled prophecy, and then not be able to give examples. Consider the predictions concerning Christ's coming, which were literally fulfilled.

He was born in Bethlehem (Micah 5:2 fulfilled in Matthew 2:1). He was of the line of David (Isaiah 11:1-5; Matthew 1:1). He was of the tribe of Judah (Genesis 49:10; Luke 3:33). He was born of a virgin (Isaiah 7:14; Matthew 1:18-23). He ministered in Zebulun in Naphtali, which is Galilee (Isaiah 9:1; Matthew 4:12-15).

He was a prophet (Deuteronomy 18:15; Acts 3:19-26). He was rejected by the Jews (Isaiah 53:3; John 1:11). He entered Jerusalem on a young donkey (Zechariah 9:9; John 12:13-15). He was sold for thirty pieces of silver (Zechariah 11:12; Matthew 26:15). He suffered for our sin (Isaiah 53:4; I Peter 2:24). He rose from the grave (Psalm 16:10; Acts 2:24-32). He ascended into heaven (Psalm 68:18; Acts 1:9-11). These are but a few of the fulfilled prophecies concerning Jesus Christ.

In his book *Science Speaks,* Peter Stoner applies the modern science of probability to just eight of the above prophecies, and states that the chances of Jesus fulfilling all eight would be one in a hundred quadrillion (that's 100,000,000,000,000,000). [32] Stoner suggests that if we were to have that many silver dollars, they would cover the entire State of Texas to a depth of two feet!

The probability of all eight prophecies being fulfilled in Jesus by chance would be like marking one of those silver dollars, then blindfolding someone and asking him to walk through the State to find that marked coin!

Jesus Christ Referred to the Old Testament with Complete Confidence That It Was the Word of God

This is yet another wonderful reason why we can have confidence in the Scriptures. Jesus quoted the Old Testament frequently, and introduced His teaching many times with the words "It is written...." He encouraged the use of the Scriptures (John 5:39), told the Pharisees they erred because they did not know them (Matthew 22:29), and endorsed them by declaring, "the Scripture cannot be broken" (John 10:35). Much of the New Testament is merely the fulfillment of what the Old Testament predicted by way of both symbols and outright declarations.

The Unity of the Bible is a Miracle

The Bible was written over a period of 1,600 years by some 40 different authors in different countries, from different backgrounds and cultures, and with little sharing of ideas. Yet it is a complete and perfect whole of truth.

Can you imagine 40 authors in different countries writing on the same subject for that length of time, yet they have such a common theme that it dovetails together as a perfect, consistent whole? No wonder the Bible holds a leading place in literature today, and has been translated into well over 1,000 languages.

Christians Have Found That the Bible Delivers on its Promises

Down through the centuries, Christians have found that when they fulfill the conditions laid down in the Bible, they receive what it promises. Millions have had their lives changed and protected by obeying the Bible's commandments. They have had their prayers answered, their needs provided, and their fears relieved.

Dr. McMillen declares that over half the diseases and sorrows of the human race would be wiped away if people would just follow the teachings of Jesus. This is quite aside from miraculous intervention in divine healing.

It is very practical to believe the Bible. When we lay hands on the sick and see them recover, and when blind eyes are opened and the deaf receive their hearing, this proves the authenticity of the teachings of Jesus Christ and the other biblical writers. And all this is quite aside from getting to know God, which is of even greater importance.

These nine reasons are not the only ones, but they should prove sufficient for the honest inquirer. There are numerous other examples that we can give apart from the ones mentioned here. Take mental and written note of them as you come across them so that you can use them at a moment's notice as you witness.

19

Saying It by Writing

For five years, I led the course on cross-cultural evangelism at the University of the Nations in Hawaii. For the first three of those years, I considered the idea of giving my students the assignment of writing a tract. But I always decided against it, feeling it might be too much for some of them. (After all, not everyone likes to write!)

Then one day I was listening to Danny Lehmann, a former surfer who used to do drugs in California before his conversion. These days, he is a noted personal evangelist, and is the leader of the Honolulu YWAM center. I had asked Danny to speak in our class for a few days. The picture of health with his blonde hair and bronzed skin, Danny enthusiastically shared his enlightening (and sometimes amusing) stories about witnessing. He is a very effective personal evangelist, and it is always a joy to listen to his teaching.

Danny is a great "tract" man, too, and usually goes out witnessing with a custom-made leather pouch strapped to his side, containing a variety of Christian leaflets kept out of sight until the right time.

During one teaching session, Danny talked about how he passes people a tract at a suitable time in his witnessing endeavors. With one particular leaflet, though, he told us that he was able to say, "This is something I wrote," as he offered it.

As he said that, lights flashed in my mind, and bells started ringing. *Of course,* I said to myself, *that's the answer!* I should get my students to write their own tract so they would be able to say, "This is something I wrote." *But instead of writing a preaching tract,* I thought, *they could just write about one aspect of their personal testimony. That shouldn't be too hard.*

And so we all did just that—staff and students alike. We wrote down what we felt was appropriate, had someone check it for content and progression of thought, and then had it typed up on a regular sheet of paper. When folded in half twice, it read like a greeting card. Once we liked what we'd typed up, we had a few copies made. And the result? Although I have handed mine out to many people over the last two years, only a couple of people have turned me down.

Perhaps the most interesting comment I've received was just after I'd been witnessing in Honolulu with a YWAM team. My partner and I were waiting at a street corner for our ride home when a prostitute walked by. I decided to hand her my testimony tract. At first she declined it, keeping her distance. But when I told her I had written it, her face lit up.

"You wrote this? Okay, I'll take it!" she said as she reached out to accept it.

About five minutes later, my partner and I were still waiting at that same corner, and who should come by but the same lady once more. This time, she walked straight up to me and declared: "That's the best thing I have ever read." Then she started explaining her situation. "I know what I'm doing is wrong," she began, "but you see, I have four children." And I was off witnessing yet again.

I believe the reason for her interest in that tract was that it was a short story about my life (even though it contained a message). She may have found it more interesting than a tract with a doctrinal emphasis.

On another occasion, a man read the first page of my tract (I intentionally only have six lines on that page) and said, "It sounds like the story of my life." Then he asked the same thing that many others have, "Can I keep it?"

Why don't you have a go at writing your own tract? If the idea appeals to you, here are a few hints.

Simply write out one slice of your testimony, keeping in mind that you will be giving this to a non-Christian. Bear in mind all the points mentioned in Chapter Four, including staying clear of church jargon. Try to keep it to one theme—emphasizing specifically what

Christ has completely changed in your life.

You'll need to keep it short if you want the one-page-folded-in-four-format. Figure out before you begin whether you want to use it as something to hand out in order to get a conversation going, or something you offer people at the end of your time together. If it is to help you engage people in conversation, then it should have a lot of your personal story, and not much about doctrine. Otherwise, you may turn people off. If you intend to give it out only after you've had a very good talk with someone, you can insert more teaching about how they can get to know God.

You will also need to consider who your target audience will be. Your content and style of language will differ, depending on whether you are writing for teenagers or for the middle-aged, for the educated or the uneducated, etc. And remember, you may have to write and rewrite your little tract over and over until you have it sounding the way you want it.

Have someone from your target audience read it, and ask for comments. If they don't understand your points clearly, thank them warmly! Those remarks are like gold, because the purpose of writing your own tract is to communicate. If someone from your target audience doesn't get your point, chances are that there are many others who won't understand your message, either. So write it out once again and have someone different check it.

Just a couple of extra cautions: Make sure someone who is spiritually mature reads what you've written before you commit it to print. A spiritually responsible person needs to check the content of your tract. If you're going to mention the name of your church anywhere, first make sure that your pastor agrees with what you've written.

I trust that many of you will respond to this challenge. Happy writing!

20

Closing Thoughts

If people ask me, "What is the single biggest piece of advice you can give about witnessing?" I would probably say it is to *be wise in your contact with the outside world.*

We must demonstrate the character of God as we live and witness for Christ. We saw the importance of this in an earlier chapter, but it bears repeating here. I once heard of a man spreading the Gospel everywhere, but none of his children were believers. His wife told me that it was because they did not see Christ in his life.

People instinctively believe that knowing God has something to do with holiness. Paul wrote, "Be wise in the way you act toward outsiders; make the most of every opportunity. *Let your conversation be always full of grace...*" (Colossians 4:5-6, italics mine).

Following are three more points I'd like to emphasize in bringing this book to a close.

The Value of the Planned and Inspirational Approaches

The witnessing guidelines described throughout this book follow a logical pattern, backed up by what is set out in Scripture. They constitute what we might call the *planned approach.* That is, we first sense if the person is comfortable with a belief in God; then move on to the subject of His character, man and his sin, Jesus Christ, repentance, and so on. But while I believe in this mapped-out path, I also feel that we should be willing to be open to any inspirational approach which God may suddenly reveal to us such as that which happened in the following story.

While witnessing in a village in India, we happened upon a Muslim lady whose husband had left her seven years earlier. Invited to talk with her further, we crowded into a tiny, one-room home. Her adult son also listened from a corner of the darkened dwelling.

I started the conversation along the lines of the planned approach this book has outlined. Speaking through an interpreter, I carefully affirmed the existence of God, in whom she already believed. Then I started talking about His character, how real He can be to us, how He communicates with us, and how He gives us a sense of His presence.

At this point, she interrupted me and blurted out, "I've been crying out to God for seven years, and He hasn't done anything for me!"

As soon as she said that, I felt God impress me with the sense that if I were to pray for her right then, she would feel His presence. Never in my long experience of witnessing had I ever felt God instill that thought in me. Neither have I heard Him say that to me since.

I told the woman what I was about to do in obedience to that prompting of God's Spirit. (Actually, this is what faith is all about. We can launch out into the unknown, and expect God to come through for us when we have first heard from Him).

I wanted to introduce this lady not only to our supernatural God, but also to our Lord Jesus Christ. But since she was a Muslim, I knew we had to introduce Jesus to her carefully. It would have to be in a way she could receive. The Koran talks about Jesus as a prophet, although we know, of course, that He is the Son of God.

So I simply said: "I'm going to pray for you in the name of the prophet Jesus." Still in the interested gaze of that 21-year-old son who was watching everything from the safety of the corner, we assembled around this lady. We asked her to clasp her hands in front of her in a pose of prayer. Not touching her except for placing our hands over hers, we prayed.

After we'd finished, she sat still, looking spellbound. When she finally broke her silence, she spoke with wonder and excitement. She said that she'd felt a burning sensation in her eyes. And in awe, she said, "I have felt the presence of God!"

I continued witnessing. I told her that the person in whose name we had prayed was not just a prophet. He was the Son of the Living God. She had no argument with that. Why should she?

She was convinced, because the name of Jesus had brought the power and the presence of God in a dimension she had never felt before. Anyone like that had to be divine!

Right then, she came to Christ. When I visited her with a local pastor some weeks later, she excitedly lifted one hand high in the air and said, "Jesus is the only God!"

This story illustrates the *inspirational approach.* So although there is a planned method, the way of being open to the leading of the Holy Spirit will complement the planned approach. Actually, any inspirational approach should not completely eclipse the planned approach, but should make it easier for the sinner to come to Christ much faster!

Start in Agreement

If we start our conversation with the unsaved in areas of mutual agreement, then move on from there, we'll find that those we're talking to will find it easy to listen to all our views.

Yet it is amazing to me how much witnessing is done today by those who actually start the conversation in an area of known disagreement. I wish to counsel you strongly against this confrontational approach, and suggest that the examples of Jesus appearing to Gulshan Esther (Chapter Six) and His approach to Sam Faet (Chapter Eight) provide us with good models.

In both instances, Jesus began speaking to them in a way they could relate to. He didn't come out with all His revelation at once. In both cases, His wisdom won the heart of His hearer, although in each instance, there was a delay in the sinner coming to faith.

Stir Yourself Often

Actually, this applies just as much to me as to anyone else. Remember to pray for those to whom we have witnessed, and ask God to improve our abilities in evangelism.

In his book *Bringin' 'Em Back Alive,* Danny Lehmann says that we can tell our highest priorities simply by gauging how much time we spend doing various activities. He continues his challenging exhortation by asking:

> How much time do you spend praying about the effectiveness of your evangelism? How often do you pray for the lost? When was the last time you prayed and fasted for someone's salvation?[33]

May God give us many people to influence for Him as we point people to Him, and as we turn conversations from the mundane to the spiritual.

In this context, remember Melville, the banker whose story I shared in the first chapter? I am happy to say that over the last twenty years, Melville has joined various Christian activities and outreaches, and recently made several trips into China carrying Bibles. In his retirement, he has worked on the release of this book into the Singhala language.

Melville's life in Christ started that day many years ago in his bank office, when I guided a mundane conversation into a spiritual one. May God lead you also into many exciting conversations for Him, and may you, too, have the thrill of leading others to Christ.

Happy witnessing!

Open Book Examination

1. What do you see as the three most compelling reasons why the vision for personal evangelism needs to be restored to the Church today?
2. Explain why personal evangelism is necessary for a well-balanced Christian life.
3. Why do you think we should be gracious as we witness?
4. What does it mean to "speak from a low position"? How should we put this into practice?
5. Explain the importance of "starting in agreement."
6. Why should our approach in evangelism depend on the sinner's attitude to the Word of God?
7. How do we know that God exists? What ways of verifying His existence would appeal to what categories of people?
8. How would you start witnessing to a member of a primitive tribe who has never heard the Gospel?
9. How do we know that Jesus is the Son of God? Give reasons from Scripture, history, logic, etc.
10. What did God intend should happen in the heart of a sinner through the Cross? Explain concisely, yet adequately.
11. Describe the things that the repentant sinner must turn from. Give references.
12. Why is it not best to ask, "Do you want to receive Jesus?" What should you say?
13. Why should we make restitution? Doesn't the blood of Jesus Christ cleanse us from all sin?
14. Before praying with someone to become a Christian, we should make sure they are repentant. What else should they consider?
15. What do you think are the three most important things to do in follow-up in a non-Western country?

16. What five things should we teach a new convert?
17. Write out what you see as the four best reasons which prove that the Bible is the Word of God. Give adequate explanation why each reason is convincing to you.
18. If you are a Westerner, identify the cultural difference that would be hardest for you to adapt to if you were to live in a non-Western country. Then think of some ways you might go about learning to accommodate that difference.

    If you are a non-Westerner, indicate the Western way which would be hardest for you to accommodate. Then write down the ways you can think of to help you make this change if you were called to witness in a Western nation.
19. What is the difference between the "planned approach" and the "inspirational approach"?
20. State that you have read this entire book.

Endnotes

1. K.K. Alavi, *In Search of Assurance* (Bombay, India: G.L.S.).
2. *Time* magazine, February 17, 1986, p. 63.
3. Brother Andrew, *Open Doors Magazine,* 1970.
4. Ralph D. Winter, "The Two Structures of God's Redemptive Mission," in *Crucial Dimensions in World Evangelization* (Pasadena, CA: William Carey Library, 1976), pp. 326-341.
5. Dorothy Baruch, *New Ways in Discipline: You and Your Child Today* (New York, NY: McGraw-Hill Book Company).
6. Winkie Pratney, *Revival* (Springdale, PA: Whitaker House, 1983), p. 175.
7. Joy Dawson, *How to Pray for Someone Near You Who is Away from God* (Seattle, WA: YWAM Publishing, 1987), pp. 4-7. Used by permission.
8. Zeus was attributed powers similar to those ascribed to the Roman god, Jupiter. But Paul could not use the term *Zeus* to describe God, because Greek theologians had begun saying that Zeus was the offspring of Kronus and Rhea. Therefore the name Zeus no longer meant "uncreated Creator."
9. Gulshan Esther, *The Torn Veil* (Fort Washington, PA 19034: CLC Books, 1989), p. 48.
10. *Cyclopedia of New Zealand,* 1897.
11. Tissa Weerasingha, *The Cross and the Bo Tree* (Taipei, Taiwan: Asia Theological Association, 1989), pp. 47-48, 90.
12. C.R. Marsh, *Share Your Faith with a Muslim* (Chicago, IL: Moody Press, 1975), p. 37.
13. Noel Gibson, *Twenty Minutes to Decide!* (Drummoyne, N.S.W. 2047, Australia: Freedom in Christ Ministries Trust, 1990), p. 15. Used by permission.
14. C.S. Lewis, *Mere Christianity* (New York: Macmillan Publishing Co., 1952) p. 17.

15. Don Richardson, *Eternity in Their Hearts* (Ventura, CA: Regal Books, 1981), pp. 43-46.
16. Taken from the *NIV Study Bible,* p. 1496. Copyright 1985 by the Zondervan Corporation. Used by permission.
17. Mel Tari, *Like a Mighty Wind* (Green Forest, AR: New Leaf Press), pp. 143-145. Used by permission.
18. Christian World Service T.V. broadcast, Conferences of Churches in Aotearoa, Box 22-652, Christchurch, New Zealand.
19. ABC World News Tonight, New York, October 20, 1992.
20. Floyd McClung, *Dead Men Don't Think,* pp. 3, 5.
21. Frank Morrison, *Who Moved the Stone* (Downer's Grove, Ill: InterVarsity Press).
22. Josephus, *Antiquities of the Jews* (Grand Rapids, Michigan: Kregel Publications, 1960), Book XVIII, Chapter 3; Section 3.
23. Joy Dawson, *How to Pray for Someone Near You Who is Away from God* (Seattle, WA: YWAM Publishing, 1987), p. 9.
24. John Sherrill, *My Friend the Bible* (originally published by Chosen Books in 1978—contact YWAM Publishing for more details). Used by permission.
25. Dr. Billy Graham; Dr. James Hodge, M.D., Emeritus Professor of Psychiatry at the Northeastern Ohio University's College of Medicine.
26. Lloyd Billingsley, "Half in Love with Easeful Death," *Eternity Magazine,* March 1985 issue, p. 28.
27. If you wish to know more about cultural differences, there are a number of books around on this subject. A classic is Marvin K. Mayers' *Christianity Confronts Culture* (Grand Rapids, MI: Zondervan, 1987). A simple introduction to the subject is Marvin K. Mayers' and Sherwood Lingenfelter's *Ministering Cross-culturally* (Grand Rapids, MI: Baker Book House, 1986).

28. Taken from the *NIV Study Bible,* p. 5. Copyright 1985 by the Zondervan Corporation. Used by permission.

29. *Thompson Chain Bible* (B.B. Kirkbride Bible Co., 1964), p. 338.

30. Paul E. Little, *Know Why You Believe* (Downers Grove, Ill: InterVarsity Press).

31. Dr. S.I. McMillen, *None of These Diseases* (Old Tappan, New Jersey: Fleming Revell, 1963).

32. Peter Stoner, *Science Speaks* (Chicago, Ill: Moody Press, 1963), p. 107.

33. Danny Lehmann, *Bringin' 'Em Back Alive* (Springdale, PA: Whitaker House, 1987), p. 31.